Study Guide

to accompany

Appelbaum and Chambliss

SOCIOLOGY

SECOND EDITION

Marilyn J. Carter
UNIVERSITY OF OREGON

 LONGMAN

An imprint of Addison Wesley Longman, Inc.

New York • Reading, Massachusetts • Menlo Park, California • Harlow, England
Don Mills, Ontario • Sydney • Mexico City • Madrid • Amsterdam

Study Guide to accompany Appelbaum and Chambliss SOCIOLOGY, Second Edition

Copyright © 1997 Longman Publishers USA, A Division of Addison Wesley Longman, Inc.

ISBN: 0-673-98184-3

97 98 99 00 01 9 8 7 6 5 4 3 2

Table of Contents

INTRODUCTION

This study guide is designed to assist your understanding of sociology, and to introduce you to the major themes presented in Appelbaum and Chambliss's **SOCIOLOGY, Second Edition**. This study guide is not a substitute for the text, but is to be used in conjunction with it. It is important that you read each chapter in your textbook carefully before tackling the work activities presented in this study guide. Some simple strategies will help you to get the most from your text and from this study guide, including: (1) previewing, (2) reading with a purpose, and (3) reviewing.

1.   **P**reviewing

- Examine the table of contents, noting headings, and subheadings.

- Read any introductory materials, such as the introduction and preface.

- Become familiar with the layout of the chapters, including special boxed features and other in-text learning aids.

- Read the title of the chapter, the headings, and subheadings.

- Read the Learning Objectives for each chapter.

- Preview the key terms.

A.   It is important to remember that what you do before and after you read a selection from your textbook is as important as the reading itself. Before you plunge into the reading, take some time to become familiar with your textbook. Look through the table of contents, noting headings and subheadings. Read any introductory materials, such as the introduction and preface, that will help you to use your text effectively and will give you a summary of the purpose, philosophy, and contents of the text. Become familiar with the layout of the chapters, including special boxed features and other in-text learning aids. In **SOCIOLOGY, Second Edition**, authors Richard Appelbaum and William Chambliss have provided *Critical Thinking* feature boxes in each chapter that ask students to consider various social issues and to respond to questions pertaining to the issues raised. By using the *Critical Thinking* boxes and other features of your text, you will be introduced to a wide-range of current issues and challenged to think critically about them.

Before reading, take a closer look at the chapter. Read the title of the chapter, the headings, and subheadings. Read the *Learning Objectives* for each chapter to get an idea of what you are expected to learn, and to become familiar with the chapter's focus and organization. It is often helpful to preview the key terms that are presented at the end of the chapter before plunging into your reading. This will acquaint you with new terms and ideas before encountering them in the text, and will help you to commit their meanings to memory.

2. Reading with a Purpose

- Read with the intention of answering questions.

- Highlight or underline key terms, important ideas, or crucial arguments.

- Make margin notes.

- Make split-page notes.

Reading effectively is more than just reading a chapter in the text. To read effectively, you should read with a purpose--that is, with the intention of answering questions. There are three strategies that I have found useful to help me get the most from my reading: highlighting and underlining, making margin notes, and making split-page notes.

A. Highlight or underline key terms, important ideas, or any major points that you want to learn. It is important that you read the section in your chapter <u>before</u> you highlight or underline it. This will enable you to identify and mark only the main or supporting points or ideas. Again, any highlighting or underlining should be done with the purpose of answering questions about the material being covered.

B. Making margin notes is another useful way to record information that you want to learn and, as with highlighting and underlining, should be done with the purpose of getting answers to questions about the material being covered. As you are reading, enumerate major points (*1, 2, 3*), identify examples that illustrate major points, crucial arguments, and jot down important names, dates, or titles. If you are reading about a particular sociological study, identify the purpose of the study and its major findings. Remember, though, too much margin notation becomes confusing and is of little value when reviewing your chapter. It is important to read through a section in the text before making any notations in the margin. After you have read the section, jot down the question that the section answers, then mark where the answer is found in the section by enumerating, bulleting, or other pointer notations.

C. Making split-page notes is another useful strategy to help you read effectively, and can be done while you are reading the chapter or after you have finished your reading. Split-page notetaking can be done in conjunction with or in place of highlighting, underling, and making margin notes. To make split-page notes, you will need notebook paper. Before beginning to read a chapter, write down the chapter title and a brief summary of its major themes. Then, draw a vertical line through the page, with one-third of the page in the left-hand column and two-thirds in the right-hand column. This split-page format will be continued on subsequent pages until you have worked through the chapter. As stated before, it is important to read through a section before taking any notes. Once you have read the section, jot down the question that the section answers in the left-hand column. Then, in the right-hand column, write the answer to that question. Be sure to list key points, major findings, or any other important information that you wish to learn. I think you will find that split-page notes are much easier to use when it comes time to review the chapter and to prepare for exams.

3. Reviewing

• Recite information that you want to learn and remember.

• Work through the review and study activities in this study guide.

After you have read your chapter, it is important that you review the material to learn it and to enable you to recall it. Reciting important information and working through this study guide are two review strategies that will assist you in learning and recalling the materials covered in the text.

A. Recitation, repeating information aloud or silently, is one valuable way to review the material that you have covered. If you have followed the question and answer format while highlighting or notetaking, it will be very easy for you to recite the information you wish to learn. If you have taken split-page notes, for example, cover the answers contained in the right-hand column, and attempt to answer the questions that you formulated for each section contained in the left-hand column. This strategy also can be used to review margin notations. One piece of advice, while it's important that you attempt to learn and remember important names, dates, and other supporting details, it is crucial that you understand the main points or arguments being made. Finally, it is also important that you use this review strategy on a regular basis. Your study time should include time for review.

B. This study guide is intended to help you understand and remember what you read in Appelbaum and Chambliss's **SOCIOLOGY, Second Edition**. Each chapter of the text is covered by a chapter in the study guide. I have followed the same format for each chapter. The *Learning Objectives* are what you should know and understand after you have read and reviewed the chapter. The *Chapter Overview* is an active, question and answer review of the materials covered in the chapter. The *Student Activities* section includes questions and activities that will assist you in learning the text material. It might also be used as a springboard for discussion with other students. The *Test Question* section contains a number of questions in various formats: multiple choice, true/false, matching, and completion. It is suggested that you read your text, using your preferred method of notetaking. Then, work through the corresponding chapter in this study guide. If you are unable to recall some of the material covered in your reading, go back to the text to help you develop answers to the questions presented in this study guide. Take the practice exams only after you have completed the chapter review.

The Appelbaum and Chambliss text is thought provoking and enjoyable. It is my hope that this study guide will enhance your understanding of sociology and to master the information presented in your text.

Marilyn J. Carter
Department of Sociology
University of Oregon

PART I

INTRODUCTION TO SOCIOLOGY

CHAPTER 1

THE SOCIOLOGICAL PERSPECTIVE

I.   LEARNING OBJECTIVES

1.   To identify the key social forces that are shaping our world today and how sociology can provide insights into them.
2.   To understand the concept of the sociological imagination.
3.   To become familiar with the nature of sociological inquiry.
4.   To understand the difference between the social and natural sciences.
5.   To understand how the science of sociology developed.
6.   To become familiar with the basic sociological perspectives: functionalism, social conflict theory, and symbolic interactionism.

CHAPTER OVERVIEW

This chapter introduces you to sociology and issue of globalization in modern sociological understanding. Working through this chapter overview will help you to recall many of the topics and issues covered in your textbook and will prepare you to take the practice tests that follow.

A.   **Sociology -- A Global Focus.** Worldwide population growth, the destruction of our planet's environment, the end of the Cold War, ethnic and racial conflicts, and worldwide health epidemics are some of the key forces shaping our world today. For this reason, the authors emphasize the importance of *globalization* as a central feature of contemporary life.

1.   Define the term *globalization*.

2.   Why is globalization important to our sociological understanding?

3.   What is sociology, and how can it provide insights into environmental, economic, or political problems?

4.   Define *critical thinking*. What critical questions might you raise about the effects of globalization on the United States or other countries?

B. **The Sociological Imagination.** Sociology is concerned with the systematic study of human beings and their social worlds. Sociologists view the world in a way that permits them to see the relationship between our personal lives and the larger social forces that shape our lives.

1. According to C. Wright Mills, *sociological imagination* refers to:

2. How might the sociological imagination help us to understand the relationship between an individual illegal act and larger social forces?

3. Discuss the distinction between the *micro* and *macro* levels of social relations.

4. A key objective of the text is to help us to understand how our daily lives are both shaped by larger historical processes and how we are the makers of history. Give an example from your text or your personal life to illustrate this point.

C. **Principal Themes in Sociological Research.** The authors pay particular attention to three themes in sociological research that are of central importance in understanding our world: diversity, inequality, and globalization.

1. Define *diversity* and explain why human diversity is important.

2. List two reasons why globalization presents a challenge to human diversity.

    a.

    b.

3. What does it mean to be *ethnocentric*?

4. Define *inequality*.

5. What does the sociological imagination reveal about the relationship between individual economic status and systematic social forces that contribute to inequality?

6. Your textbook discusses many of the ways in which increased globalization has brought about changes in the American economy, politics, popular culture, and the environment. Give an example from your textbook or from personal experience illustrating the effect of increased globalization.

D. **Sociology and Science.** While the sociological imagination can reveal much about the ways in which our lives as individuals are affected by larger social forces, it is another matter to link specific observations in a meaningful way. To do this, both social and natural scientists rely on systematic theory and observation to provide explanations of how things work.

1. How do the authors define *scientific theory* and its relationship to *scientific research*?

2. What are the six characteristics of a good theory?

    _____   _____   _____

    _____   _____   _____

3. The authors identify several important differences between the social and natural sciences. List four of those differences below.

    a.

    b.

    c.

    d.

4. The authors list five social science disciplines. Beginning with sociology, list the social science disciplines below, and identify their respective objects of study.

	Discipline	Object of Study
a.	_____	_____
b.	_____	_____

c. _____   _____

d. _____   _____

e. _____   _____

5.   What is the underlying assumption that makes sociology unique among the social scientific disciplines?

6.   The authors define scientific theories as sets of logically consistent assumptions or ideas about the relationship between things. In attempting to develop theories, sociologists are faced with determining the problems to be investigated and how to go about studying them. To assist them in developing theories about the way the world works, sociologists organize their work by using one or more of three major paradigms.

    a.   Define the term *paradigm*.

    b.   List the three major paradigms of sociology and state whether they are concerned with micro-level or macro-level social processes:

<u>Paradigm</u>	<u>Level of Focus</u>
(1)	
(2)	
(3)	

    c.   Each of the major paradigms of sociology has a particular way of viewing society and the nature of social relations. State how each paradigm views society.

        (1) Functionalist Paradigm

        (2) Social Conflict Paradigm

4

(3) Symbolic Interactionist Paradigm

    d.   Using the chart below, identify how each of these paradigms might explain the role of schools and education in society.

          <u>Paradigm</u>   <u>Explanation</u>

(1)

(2)

(3)

E.   **The Emergence of Sociological Theory**. Sociology is a relatively young academic discipline--much younger than physics or history, for example. Sociology arose in nineteenth century Europe in response to the sweeping changes ushered in with the emergence of the modern era.

    1.   List the three historical events that contributed to the rise of sociology.

        a.

        b.

        c.

    2.   List the four founders of sociology and the paradigm with which they are identified. Then, in the space provided, briefly discuss some of their main ideas.

           <u>Founders</u>   <u>Paradigm</u>

        a. _____   _____
        Main Ideas:

        b. _____   _____
        Main Ideas:

c. _____   _____

Main Ideas:

d. _____   _____

Main Ideas:

3.   Give two reasons to explain why women and people of color are absent from historical accounts of the origin of sociology?

a.

b.

4.   Briefly discuss the contributions to sociology made by the following scholars:

a.   Harriet Martineau (1802-1876)

b.   Ida B. Wells-Barnett (1862-1931)

5.   American sociology emerged in the early twentieth century with the rapid rise of industrialization and urbanization. The authors tell us that many American sociologists were activists and took up the problems and causes of those in society who were exploited or oppressed.

a.   What is the name of first academic department devoted entirely to sociology and what was the department's primary focus of research? Give one or two examples illustrating the sort of research coming out of the newly founded department.

b.   Who was W. E. B. DuBois (1868-1963), and what was the focus of his path breaking sociological research?

c.   Although she never achieved full recognition by the discipline, what lasting contributions did Jane Addams (1860-1935) make to sociology?

d.   What changes took place within American sociology after World War II?

e.   Define Robert K. Merton's (1910-) *manifest functions* and *latent functions* and discuss how they contribute to the functionalist paradigm.

III.   STUDENT ACTIVITIES

1.   Sports are an important part of American social life and throughout the world. How would you, as a *Functionalist sociologist*, explain the role of sports in modern society? In responding, consider the manifest and latent functions of sports.

Now, how would you, as a *Social Conflict sociologist*, explain the role of sports in modern society? In responding, consider how participation in sports discriminates on the basis of sex, race, and economic factors.

Finally, how would you, as a *Symbolic Interactionist sociologist*, explain the role of sports in modern society? In responding, consider how a sports event is achieved through the social interaction of the participants involved.

2.   The authors stress the importance of *globalization* in our sociological understanding. Locate six cartoons or news items that illustrate the positive and negative effects of globalization.   In locating your cartoons or news items, consider the promises and problems globalization holds for human diversity, the American economy, politics, popular culture, and the environment.

3.   We have learned that the *sociological imagination* allows us to see the relationship between our individual lives and the larger social forces that shape our lives. First, list two or three reasons why you attend your particular college. Now, taking a step back from your individual life experience, how would you as a sociologist explain your college participation? In responding, consider what you and other students have in common as a category of people--age, race, and income, for example.

IV.   KEY TERMS

Listed below are some of the key terms that are introduced in Chapter 1. After you have read Chapter 1 in your text and worked through the overview of Chapter 1 on the preceding pages, test your recall by writing the definitions of the terms in the space provided. You may check your work by referring to the *Key Terms* section at the end of the chapter in your text.

Anomie _____

_____

Critical thinking _____

_____

Ethnocentric _____

_____

Globalization _____

_____

Functionalist paradigm _____

_____

Ideal types _____

_____

Macro-level _____

_____

Micro-level _____

_____

Paradigm _____

_____

Positivism _____

_____

Scientific theory _____

_____

Social class _____

_____

Social conflict paradigm _____

_____

Sociological imagination _____

_____

Symbolic Interactionist paradigm _____

_____

V. TEST QUESTIONS

Multiple-Choice Questions
Choose the correct answer from the choices provided.

1. Which of the following is a characteristic of sociology?
    a. It is interested in how people create and change their social world.
    b. It assumes that social relationships hold the key to understanding how social life operates.
    c. It uses scientific research methods.
    d. all of the above

2. Which of the early sociologists emphasized the importance of ideal types and bureaucracies in modern society?
    a. Karl Marx
    b. Max Weber
    c. Emile Durkheim
    d. Auguste Comte

3. Karl Marx believed that:
    a. the task of the social scientist was solely to interpret the world.
    b. capitalism was a new type of social order that would satisfy the needs of everyone.
    c. capitalism divides people into two competing groups with conflicting interests.
    d. societies of his day would be transformed by changing cultural values.

4. A sociological study at the *macro-level* of analysis might focus on:
    a. how people interact in telephone conversations.
    b. how suicide rates vary over time.
    c. discrimination based on race or ethnicity.
    d. both b and c

5. Which of the following sociologists coined the term *sociological imagination?*
    a. C. Wright Mills
    b. Auguste Comte
    c. Max Weber
    d. W. E. B. DuBois

6. Which of the following sociologists is credited with founding sociology?
    a. Charles Horton Cooley
    b. Emile Durkheim
    c. Auguste Comte
    d. Karl Marx

7. The Functionalist paradigm is concerned primarily with:
   a. conflict and social change.
   b. social structure and how society remains stable over time.
   c. micro-level interaction.
   d. how individuals actively construct a sense of self and society.

8. The sociological imagination refers to:
   a. the use of scientific theory and research methods to explain social phenomena.
   b. the ability to see how our individual lives are influenced by larger social forces.
   c. the ability to understand the subjective experience of the people being studied.
   d. the ability to imagine and create a better world.

9. After World War II, American sociology shifted to a greater emphasis on:
   a. social problems.
   b. micro-level analyses.
   c. statistical modeling of social processes.
   d. macro-level analyses.

10. The sociological paradigm that focuses on micro-level processes is:
    a. Functionalist paradigm.
    b. Social Conflict paradigm.
    c. Symbolic Interactionist paradigm.
    d. none of the above.

True/False Questions
For each of the following statements, decide whether the statement is true or false. Write your answer in the space provided.

_____ 1. American sociology originated in the midwest in the early twentieth century and focused on the problems brought about by industrialization and urbanization.

_____ 2. Max Weber believed that an adequate explanation of the social world must begin with the individual.

_____ 3. A sociologist working within the Functionalist paradigm would probably approach a study of education in America by examining who benefits and who does not benefit from the existing educational system.

_____ 4. Early sociologist, Emile Durkheim, sought to explain suicide in terms of social facts.

_____ 5. Women and people of color are absent from historical accounts of sociology's origins because they did not begin conducting sociological research until the twentieth century.

_____ 6. Karl Marx emphasized the negative consequences of capitalism for the lives of working people and sought to develop a theory of social change to bring about its downfall.

_____ 7. A sociologist working within the Social Conflict paradigm would most likely emphasize the importance of religious beliefs and values in explaining the emergence of capitalism.

_____ 8. W. E. B. DuBois was an early American sociologist who called for the scientific study of race and race relations.

_____ 9. Symbolic Interactionists are largely concerned with the study of large-scale, macro-level social processes.

_____ 10. Sociology is centrally concerned with the study of social relations, groups, and societies.

Matching Exercise
For each of the following terms, identify the correct definition and write the appropriate letter in the space provided.

a.   embeddedness
b.   ethnocentric
c.   eurocentric
d.   functionalism
e.   globalization
f.   paradigm
g.   scientific theory
h.   social conflict
i.   sociological imagination
j.   symbolic interactionism

_____ 1. a set of logically consistent ideas about the relationships between things that permit those ideas to be checked out against observations made through scientific research.

_____ 2. a sociological paradigm that focuses on how the self and society are the result of social interaction.

_____ 3. the idea that economic, political, and others forms of human activity are fundamentally shaped by social relations.

_____ 4. a term developed by C. Wright Mills that refers to the ability to see the relationship between our personal experiences and larger social forces.

_____ 5. a sociological paradigm that seeks to explain social organization and change in terms of the roles and functions performed by individual members, groups, institutions, and social relations.

_____ 6. knowledge that is centered on European-American concerns and beliefs.

_____ 7. a sociological paradigm that seeks to explain social organization and change in terms of conflict that is built into social relations.

_____ 8. a framework containing assumptions about the world that helps shape scientific theory.

_____ 9. the processes by which the lives of people around the world are increasingly interconnected.

_____ 10. the tendency to judge other cultures by one's own cultural standards and values.

Completion
Write in the word(s) that best completes each of the following statements. To check your work, you may refer to the answer key at the end of this study guide.

_____ 1. _____ is a term that refers to the state of confusion that occurs when people lose sight of the shared rules and values that give order and meaning to their lives.

_____ 2. A _____ is something understood as representing something else to the human mind, e.g., language, non-verbal gestures.

_____ 3. _____ _____ is a form of thinking characterized by a willingness to ask any question, no matter how difficult.

_____ 4. For Emile Durkheim, _____ _____ are qualities of groups that are external to individual members of society yet constrain their thinking and behavior.

_____ 5. In Robert K. Merton's theory, _____ _____ are social consequences that are *not* intended or expected by the actor, and _____ _____ are social consequences that *are* intended by the actor.

_____ 6. Three themes of sociological research that are emphasized by the authors are: _____, _____, and _____.

_____ 7. Although largely ignored by the discipline, early American sociologist W. E. B. DuBois called for the scientific sociological study of _____ _____.

_____ 8. According to Max Weber, _____ _____ are sets of sociological ideas that capture the essential features of some aspect of social reality.

_____ 9. _____-level processes involve direct social interaction with others, whereas _____-level processes refer to large-scale, more remote social processes.

_____ 10. According to Karl Marx, a conflicting relationship exists between the _____, those who own the means of production, and the _____, those who provide the labor for the operation of factories.

CHAPTER 2

THE PROCESS OF INQUIRY

I.   LEARNING OBJECTIVES

1.   To understand the differences between scientific inquiry and other ways of understanding our social world.
2.   To become familiar with the concepts of sociological research.
3.   To become familiar with the various sociological research methods and their advantages and disadvantages.
4.   To learn the stages of conducting sociological research--from defining a research problem to communicating research results to others.
5.   To become aware of some of the ethical implications of social research.

II.   CHAPTER OVERVIEW

This chapter introduces you to the process of social scientific inquiry. Basic terms and concepts of social research, various types of research methods, the process of conducting sociological inquiry, and the ethical implications of social research are discussed.

A.   **Sociological Understanding, Falsification, and Common Sense.**   While faith and common sense play an important part in our everyday thinking, sociological understanding requires that all biases, assumptions, and conclusions be put to the test.

   1.   A central difference between sociological thought and faith or common sense is that in sociology all truth claims are put to the test--that is, they can be falsified. What is the *principle of falsification*?

   2.   One of the tasks of sociological research is to develop concepts that accurately describe and measure social phenomena. Define and give an example of a sociological *concept*? How does a sociological concept differ from common sense? What does it mean to *operationally define* a concept?

   3.   What is an *hypothesis*? What is its relationship to theory?

4.   Sociologists are concerned with the *validity* and *reliability* of their research results.

    a.   Define the term *validity.*

    b.   Define the term *reliability.*

    c.   Explain and give an example illustrating how an invalid measure of a concept may be reliable in some circumstances.

5.   Define the term *variable.* Then, in the space provided, list and give an example illustrating the two types of varibles discussed in your text.

<u>Variable</u>	<u>Definition</u>	<u>Example</u>
a. *Dependent*		
b. *Independent*		

6.   Define the term *correlation,* and create a simple line graph showing the relationship between student exam scores and hours spent studying.

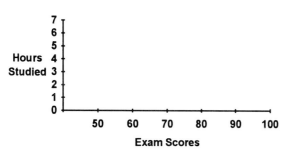

Hours Studied & Exam Scores

Hours	Scores
4	70
2	50
5	80
6	90
7	100
3	60

    a.   Does the graph show a relationship between hours students spent studying and their exam scores?

    b.   Do you think there is a *causal relationship* between hours spent studying and exam scores? Why or why not? In this example, which of the two variables is the *independent variable* and which is the *dependent variable?*

B.   **The Problem of Objectivity.** Objectivity in sociological research refers to the effort researchers make to truthfully represent their objects of study.

1.   Max Weber argued that sociological research should be *value neutral*. Define the term *value neutral*, and explain why objectivity is a problem for social scientists.

2.   What are the three ways to best achieve objectivity in social research?

a.

b.

c.

C.   **Conducting Sociological Inquiry.** Sociologists follow a *research strategy* or plan to guide their work and to answer research questions. A research strategy will suggest certain *research methods* to be used to gather data.

1.   *Survey Research*

a.   Describe survey research, and specify when it is an appropriate research method to use.

b.   What is a *population universe*?

c.   What is a *sample*, and what is its relationship to a population universe? List and define the two types of sampling mentioned in your text.

Types of sampling	Definition
(1)	
(2)	

d.   List some of the main advantages and disadvantages of survey research.

Advantages	Disadvantages
_____	_____
_____	_____

_____   _____

2. *Fieldwork*

a. Describe fieldwork or *ethnography*, and specify when it is an appropriate research method to use.

b. List some of the main advantages and disadvantages of fieldwork.

Advantages	Disadvantages
_____	_____
_____	_____
_____	_____

c. There are a number of techniques that can be used when conducting fieldwork. List the techniques discussed in your text, and describe when they are most appropriate to use.

Technique	When appropriate

(1)

(2)

(3)

3. *Participatory Research*

a. Describe participatory research, and specify when it is an appropriate research method to use.

b. Give an example illustrating how participatory research might be used to bring about social change.

c. List some of the main advantages and disadvantages of participatory research.

Advantages	Disadvantages
_____	_____
_____	_____

4. *Experiments*

    a.   What is an experiment? When it is an appropriate research method to use?

    b.   What part do *experimental groups* and *control groups* play in conducting an experiment?

    c.   List some of the main advantages and disadvantages of experiments in conducting social research.

Advantages	Disadvantages
_____	_____
_____	_____
_____	_____

    d.   What is a *field experiment*? What are some of the advantages and disadvantages to conducting field experiments as compared to laboratory experiments?

5. *Working with Available Information*

    a.   What does it mean to work with available information? When is this an appropriate research method to use?

    b.   List and identify the source(s) of the different types of available data that may be used for conducting social research. Specify the primary advantages and disadvantages of each type of available data.

Data	Source(s)
(1) _____	_____

Advantages/Disadvantages: _____
_____

	Data	Source(s)
(2)	_____	_____

Advantages/Disadvantages: _____

_____

	Data	Source(s)
(3)	_____	_____

Advantages/Disadvantages: _____

_____

    e.   What is *comparative-historical* research?

6.   *How Intrusive Should You Be?* The research methods used for sociological inquiry intrude on people's lives to varying degrees. While some methods are less intrusive than others, it is important to understand the impact social research has on the persons being studied and on the research results.

    a.   What is an *unobstrusive measure*?

    b.   List some of the ways in which the various research methods might impact the persons being studied.

    c.   Define the *Hawthorne effect*, and briefly describe how the field experiment affected the people being studied.

D.   **Doing Sociology: A Student Guide to Research.** Most sociological research goes though several stages. List the stages of sociological inquiry, and describe the tasks associated with each.

	Research Stage	Tasks
a.		
b.		
c.		
d.		
e.		

f.

g.

2. Briefly explain how the first stage of sociological inquiry--defining your research question--can exclude the experiences of some groups of people.

E. **Ethical Concerns.** All research concerned with human beings can pose ethical problems. We have already seen the importance of objectivity in conducting sociological research. Sociologists must also strive to protect the rights, privacy, and safety of research subjects.

1. What is *informed consent*?

2. Define *deception*, and state whether you think deception was warranted in Philip Goldberg's (1968) study of anti-female bias in students' evaluation of scholarly articles.

3. What does it mean to guarantee *anonymity* to the subjects of a study?

III. STUDENT ACTIVITIES

1. State a research question. Which research method(s) would you use? Why? What are the advantages and disadvantages to using your research method(s)? Does your research question or method(s) pose any ethical problems? What steps can you take to protect the rights, privacy, and safety of your subjects?

2. Your text lists a number of common sense ideas that are commonly believed to be true, but are actually false. Conduct an informal survey of ten people to test their beliefs. To do so, construct a simple questionnaire of close-ended questions/statements. For example:

   M F   Sex
   T F   Americans are among the best-educated people on earth.
   T F   Hard work and education will always pay off.

To see if there are differences in responses between males and females, you might also ask your respondents to identify their sex. After you have administered your questionnaire to your ten respondents, summarize the results of your survey.

IV. KEY TERMS

Listed below are some of the key terms that are introduced in Chapter 2. After you have read the chapter in your text and worked through the overview on the preceding pages, test your recall by writing the definitions of the terms in the space provided. You may check your work by referring to the *Key Terms* section at the end of the chapter in your text.

Applied sociology_____

_____

Concept _____

_____

Construct validity _____

_____

Correlation _____

_____

Deception _____

_____

Falsification _____

_____

Hypothesis _____

_____

Hawthorne effect _____

_____

Population universe _____

_____

Reliability _____

_____

Research methods _____

_____

Replication _____

_____

Survey ____ _____

_____

Validity_____

_____

Variable _____

_____

V. TEST QUESTIONS

Multiple-Choice Questions
Choose the correct answer from the choices provided.

1. Defining a concept in terms of the measurements that can be performed on it is called:
   a. variable assignment.
   b. conceptual assignment.
   c. labelling a variable.
   d. operationalizing.

2. A propostion that predicts a particular relationship between two or more variables and is capable of being disproved when tested is called a(n):
   a. hypothesis.
   b. theory.
   c. generalization.
   d. concept.

3. _____ refers to results that systematically misrepresent the true nature of what is being studied.
   a. Measurement error
   b. Bias
   c. Construct validity
   d. Sampling error

4. For sociological ideas to be scientific, they must be capable of:
   a. proof.
   b. falsification.
   c. changing commonly held beliefs.
   d. being experimentally tested.

5. Which of the following is a common problem confronting researchers who study the social world?
   a. The study of the social world lacks the precision of the physical sciences.
   b. The presence of an investigator may affect the behavior of the persons being studied.
   c. The investigator's involvment in the social world may diminish the objectivity of the study.
   d. all of the above

6. A scale designed to measure social class yields different results each time it is used with the same population. This shows that the scale:
   a. is biased.
   b. needs replication.
   c. lacks reliability.
   d. lacks validity.

7. A researcher wants to study the lifestyles of members of a commune by living with them for a period of time and observing their habits. This research is best characterized as:
   a. participant observation.
   b. detached observation.
   c. participatory research.
   d. a field experiment.

8. A researcher studying telephone calls to an emergency 911 number finds that participants actively construct their interactions to form coherent sequences. This sort of research is called:
   a. participant observation.
   b. biographical research.
   c. conversation analysis.
   d. evaluation research.

9. The people to whom the researcher wishes to generalize the results of a study are called the:
   a. probability sample.
   b. random sample.
   c. population universe.
   d. respondents.

10. In an experiment, the group that receives a treatment or some special attention is called the:
    a. control group.
    b. independent group.
    c. dependent group.
    d. experimental group.

True/False Questions
For each of the following statements, decide whether the statement is true or false. Write your answer in the space provided.

_____ 1. The difference between common sense and sociological concepts is that the latter are subject to scientific examination.

_____ 2. Social science research never involves deception.

_____ 3. An invalid measure of a concept cannot be reliable.

_____ 4. Participatory research is an appropriate research strategy when a primary goal is to empower people in a community or organization to conduct their own research.

_____ 5. The laboratory experiment is a particularly useful research method to study the social world.

_____ 6. Analysis of existing documents, government statistics, and historical materials are examples of unobtrusive research methods.

_____ 7. Objectivity can be a problem for sociologists because they are often studying groups of which they are members.

_____ 8. Survey research is most appropriate when first-hand knowledge of the direct experience of subjects is desired.

_____ 9. Max Weber argued that one's values and beliefs can and should enter into the selection of a topic for study, but that researchers should remain value neutral in conducting their research.

_____ 10. Correlation and causal relationship are essentially the same thing.

Matching Exercise

For each of the following terms, identify the correct definition and write the appropriate letter in the space provided.

a. causal relationship
b. deception
c. ethnography
d. informed consent
e. objectivity
f. replication
g. statistics
h. structured interviews
i. validity
j. value neutrality

_____ 1. notifying subjects of the nature of the research, any physical or psychological dangers, and the uses to which the results will be put.

_____ 2. when one variable is found to cause an effect in another variable.

_____ 3. the belief that research should not be influenced by one's personal beliefs and opinions.

_____ 4. the ability, during research, to represent the object of study as truthfully as possible.

_____ 5. a science concerned with generalizing from samples to larger populations.

_____ 6. the extent to which a concept and its measurement accurately represent what they claim to.

_____ 7. fieldwork in which researchers immerse themselves in the life of another culture to study its language and customs.

_____ 8. a research technique in which a researcher uses a detailed list of specific questions to ask respondents.

_____ 9. repetition of a previous study to verify or refute the original findings.

_____ 10. when the people being studied are not fully informed of the nature or purposes of the study.

Completion
Write in the word(s) that best completes each of the following statements. To check your work, you may refer to the answer key at the end of this study guide.

1. A sociologist discovers a causal relationship between students' social class background and their achievement in school. In this example, student achievement is the _____ variable.

2. A _____ is an abstraction that stands for properties common to a set of phenomena.

3. The categories of male and female are examples of _____ variables.

4. When two variables regularly vary together, they are said to be _____ .

5. When the relationship between two variables is actually the result of something else that is not being measured, the association is said to be _____ .

6. The research method that entails the analysis of written materials produced by individuals, government agencies, private organizations, and other sources is called _____ .

7.   In an effort to achieve objectivity in social research, researchers often invite others to draw their own conclusions about their data. This practice is referred to as _____.

8.   A _____ maps the plan for social inquiry, while a _____ refers to the specific techniques by which data is gathered.

9.   A researcher studying the similarities and differences between countries over time is most likely conducting _____ research.

10.   In a study designed to find out how to make a group of women workers increase their productivity, Roethlisberger and Dickson (1939) found that attention from the researchers affect the research results. This discovery is referred to as the _____.

PART II

THE INDIVIDUAL AND SOCIETY

CHAPTER 3

CULTURE

I.   LEARNING OBJECTIVES

1.   To understand the nature of culture and the role it plays in accounting for social conformity as well as individual differences.
2.   To understand the extent to which human culture is biologically based.
3.   To understand the role of language in shaping our perceptions of reality.
4   To appreciate the difference and relationship between material and non-material culture.
5.   To become familiar with the various aspects of cultural diversity, including subculture, counterculture, assimilation and multiculturalism, and ethnocentrism.
6.   To understand the implications of globalization on different cultures.

II.   CHAPTER OVERVIEW

One of the tasks of sociology is to enable better understanding of different cultures. This chapter introduces you to the nature of culture, the central role culture plays in shaping people's lives, and the affects of globalization on different cultures.

A.   **The Nature of Culture.** What is culture? While we often talk about culture, we rarely stop to consider what culture consists of or how it shapes our lives.

      1.   Define the term *culture* as used by sociologists and anthropologists. What exactly are the "beliefs, behaviors, and products" that make up culture?

      2.   Define the concept of *institutions*, and list some of the institutions found in society.

      3.   Define *high culture* and *popular culture*. List two or three examples of each that illustrate the distinction between the two.

      4.   What is *cultural capital*? Briefly explain how it can help a person to get ahead in society?

5.   How is *society* defined? What is the relationship between society and culture?

6.   Give two or three examples illustrating how our lives and personalities are constructed out of our shared culture? What does it mean to say that culture is a source of conformity?

B.   The Emergence and Development of Culture

1.   Briefly explain how human evolution is tied to the evolution of culture?

C.   Is There a Biological Basis for Human Culture.

1.   How do *sociobiologists* explain cultural and behavioral differences that are found between human societies? How do *social learning theorists* explain cultural and behavioral differences that are found between human societies? Which viewpoint do sociologists tend to adhere to?

2.   What are *cultural universals*? List some of the cultural universals that are found in all societies. Give an example illustrating how the expression of a cultural universal can vary from culture to culture.

D..   Aspects of Culture. In this section, you will become familiar with *material culture* and *non-material culture*.

1.   What is *material culture*? Give some examples of material culture?

2.   Explain how material culture shapes our physical options and opportunities.

3.   *Technology* is one of the most important aspects of material culture. Define *technology*.

4.	Explain how technology and other forms of material culture are becoming globalized. Provide an example illustrating the globalization of material culture. What explanation do your authors provide for the increased globalization of material culture?

5.	What is *non-material culture*? Give two or three examples of non-material.

6.	What are *values*?

7.	Contrast how *Functionalist* and *Social Conflict* sociologists regard values?

8.	What did Robert K. Merton believe were the most important values in U.S. society?

9.	Research has shown that many American values have changed over time. Give two examples of American values that have changed between 1970 and 1990. What forces contribute to changing values?

10.	What is *cultural lag*? Give an example from your text or from personal experience illustrating how cultural lag can contribute to contradictions between different values.

11.	Define the concept *norms*? List in order of increasing severity and characterize the four types of norms presented in your text. Provide an example of each norm.

<u>Norm</u>   <u>Characteristics</u>   <u>Example</u>

a.

b.

c.

d.

12.   What does it mean to *internalize* norms and values?

13.   Symbols and language characterize a culture and play a central role in our sociological understanding of different cultures.

        a.   In Chapter 1, the term *symbol* was defined as anything that represents something else to the human mind. Explain why language is an important form of symbolization in human culture.

        b.   What is the *linguistic relativity hypothesis*, and who developed it? How does language contribute to the perceptions we hold about reality?

        c.   Explain why controversies over language might increase with increased globalization.

E.   **Cultural Diversity.** Chapter 1 dealt with the importance of human diversity in the maintenance of our social world and how human diversity is challenged by increased globalization. This section deals with the importance of cultural diversity to the modern world.

    1.   Define *cultural diversity*, and explain the common misconception that sociologists have about a culture.

    2.   What is a *subculture*? Give an example of a subculture, and explain how it is distinct from the dominant culture. Is this a *hyphenated* group? Why or why not?

3.   What is a *counterculture*? Give an example of a counterculture, and explain how it is in opposition to the dominant culture.

4.   Your text offers two viewpoints concerning the experience of ethnic groups in the United States. Contrast *assimilation* and *multiculturalism*. Give examples illustrating each.

5.   In Chapter 1, *ethnocentrism* was defined as the tendency to judge other cultures by the standards of one's own culture. Define the term *cultural relativism*, and explain how it offers an alternative to ethnocentrism.

F.   **Globalization: Will a single global culture emerge?**

1.   What is *cultural diffusion*, and what part does globalization play in increasing cultural diffusion? How has cultural diffusion affected the Yanomamö peoples of Brazil and Venezuela?

2.   What are some of the *globalizing* forces that are shaping and reshaping modern culture?

3.   Define and briefly explain how globalization has contributed to a resurgence of *local cultures*.

III.   STUDENT ACTIVITIES

1.   Culture is an important source of conformity. In what ways do you conform to cultural expectations? Consider, for example, your daily schedule, the way you dress, how you behave in various situations, what and when you eat, the music that you listen to, and so forth.

2.   Give an example of a subculture. What are the characteristics--for example, dress, language, behavior--that make this subculture distinct from the dominate culture? What American values or norms does this subculture subscribe to or reject?

3.　　Increased globalization has brought people together from many different cultures who carry with them their own cultural values, norms, and ways of life. Give an example of an ethnic group, other than your own, that exists in your city. Identify a cultural value or norm held by this group that is at odds with the norms of dominant American culture. Do you think that you, as a sociologist, would be able to suspend judgment and take a cultural relativist standpoint toward this group? Why or why not?

IV.　KEY TERMS

Listed below are some of the key terms that are introduced in Chapter 3. After you have read the chapter in your text and worked through the overview on the preceding pages, test your recall by writing the definitions of the terms in the space provided. You may check your work by referring to the *Key Terms* section at the end of the chapter in your text.

Assimilation _____

_____

Cultural diffusion _____

_____

Cultural lag_____

_____

Cultural relativism _____

_____

Ideal culture _____

_____

Institutions _____

_____

Internalization _____

_____

Laws_____

_____

Material culture _____

_____

Multiculturalism _____

_____

Nationalism _____

_____

Non-material culture _____

_____

Norms_____

_____

Real culture _____

_____

Values _____

_____

V.   TEST QUESTIONS

Multiple-Choice Questions
Choose the correct answer from the choices provided.

1.   Culture is made up of:
    a.   norms.
    b.   values.
    c.   material products.
    d.   all of the above

2.   Which of the following contributed to the evolution of human culture?
    a.   human biological traits
    b.   environmental factors
    c.   symbolic communication
    d.   all of the above

3.   Social learning theorists believe that:
    a.   there is no genetic basis for behavior.
    b.   specific behaviors are the result of social factors that condition and modify biological predispositions.
    c.   that all societies contain certain cultural universals.
    d.   all of the above.

4.   All societies contain the following cultural universals:
    a.   language
    b.   norms governing childhood socialization
    c.   dance and music
    d.   all of the above

5.   Material culture consists of:
    a.   physical objects that are produced by the members of a particular society.
    b.   values.
    c.   laws.
    d.   institutions.

6. Cultural lag is:
    a. when a person is slow to learn the norms of a particular culture.
    b. when the norms of one culture change at a slower rate than another.
    c. when different parts of nonmaterial culture change at different rates in response to change in material culture.
    d. none of the above.

7. Central U.S. values that have been identified by sociologists include:
    a. the value of hard work.
    b. the capacity of science and technology to solve all of our problems.
    c. a desire for community.
    d. all of the above.

8. A person who makes offensive racial slurs to a group of African American college students is most likely violating a:
    a. law.
    b. taboo.
    c. more.
    d. folkway.

9. The norms of a particular society are obeyed because:
    a. they are internalized by members of the society through the process of socialization.
    b. normative behavior is rewarded.
    c. gossip and other informal forms of punishment enforce conformity.
    d. all of the above.

10. Nonmaterial culture consists of:
    a. physical objects that are produced.
    b. language, values, beliefs, and institutions.
    c. the technologies that are used in a society.
    d. the places where people worship.

True/False Questions
For each of the following statements, decide whether the statement is true or false. Write your answer in the space provided.

_____ 1. Most sociologists and anthropologists believe that American culture is fundamentally better than other cultures.

_____ 2. One of sociology's central insights is that our lives and personalities are constructed out of our shared culture.

_____ 3. Culture and society are the same thing.

_____ 4. Culture is an important source of conformity.

_____ 5. Sociobiologists believe that there are genetic bases for behaviors that are found among many cultures.

_____ 6. The primary difference between a subculture and a counterculture is that a counterculture generally develops in opposition to the dominant culture.

_____ 7. Robert K. Merton argued that success, prestige, wealth, and power were the most important values in the U.S.

_____ 8. Taboos are weakly held norms, whose violation is not considered serious within a particular culture.

_____ 9. Symbols are written or unwritten, verbal or nonverbal representations of things that are not immediately present to our senses.

_____ 10. Sociologists believe that the English language is the only pure language in existence today.

Matching Exercise

For each of the following terms, identify the correct definition and write the appropriate letter in the space provided.

a. assimilation
b. cultural diversity
c. folkways
d. ideal culture
e. instincts
f. internalization
g. linguistic relativity hypothesis
h. real culture
i. nationalism
j. taboo

_____ 1. biologically fixed patterns of action.

_____ 2. strongly-held norms whose violation is forbidden.

_____ 3. the process by which different cultures are absorbed into a single culture.

_____ 4. the variety of human cultural differences between and within countries.

37

_____ 5. the process by which norms and values become ingrained as ways of thinking and acting.

_____ 6. the belief that the people of a particular nation have historical or God-given rights that supersede those of any other people.

_____ 7. weak norms whose violation is generally not considered serious within a particular culture.

_____ 8. the norms and values society professes to hold.

_____ 9. the notion that perceptions are relative to language.

_____ 10. the norms and values that a society follows in practice.

Completion
Write in the word(s) that best completes each of the following statements. To check your work, you may refer to the answer key at the end of this study guide.

1. _____ refers to all of the beliefs, behaviors, and products common to members of a particular group, while _____ refers to any group of people who speak a common language, share common beliefs, belong to the same institutions, use the same tools, and consume the same goods.

2. Forms of culture that are pursued by large numbers of middle and working class people, such as spectator sports and rock music, are referred to as _____.

3. _____ argue that human beings are social in nature and that specific behaviors are always learned within a cultural context.

4. A baby automatically "rooting" for its mother's nipple or an adult withdrawing a hand from a hot stove are examples of _____.

5. _____ is defined as the practical application of knowledge, through tools and techniques, to multiply and conserve human energy.

6. _____ refers to the tendency for different parts of non-material culture to change at different rates in response to changes in material culture.

7. _____ is one of the most powerful forms of symbolization and a central feature of all human cultures.

8. A group of young people that centers around a particular type of music or exhibits a distinctive style of dress, language, and behavior is an example of a _____.

9. The _____ or "melting pot" viewpoint calls for respecting cultural differences, rather than seeking to merge all subcultures into the larger culture.

10. The influence and spread of one culture's characteristics to another--as with the Yanomamö's use of tools made in the U.S. or Japan--is referred to as _____.

CHAPTER 4

SOCIETIES

I.   LEARNING OBJECTIVES

1. To become better acquainted with the sociological concept "society" and the principal types of society that have existed throughout history.
2. To define and explain the basic terms and concepts that sociologists use to study social structure.
3. To become familiar with the major technological revolutions described by sociologists: agricultural, industrial, and the emergence of postindustrial society.
4. To understand how globalization is contributing to the convergence and transformation of the world's societies.

II.   CHAPTER OVERVIEW

In Chapter 3 you were introduced to the concepts of culture and society, and how they are understood in terms of one another. In this chapter you will learn more about the societies that have existed throughout history and about the changes that have taken place as a result of increased globalization.

A.   **What is a society?** Your text defines *society* as the interacting people who share a common culture. In this section, you will take a closer look at the concept of society to determine what constitutes a society and what does not.

    1.   The notion of *shared territory* once helped to define society. Explain why shared territory is no longer viable in the definition of society.

    2.   What part does globalization play in the definition of society?

B.   **Social Structure.** In Chapter 1, *social structure* was defined as the underlying regularities in the way people behave and interrelate with one another. In this section you will become familiar with the terms and concepts that sociologists use to study social structures that are found in different societies.

    1.   Define and give an example illustrating the concept of *structural contradiction*.

2.   *Institutions* are defined as the relatively stable rules that govern social activities in a society, and which provide shared understandings of those activities. What are some of the institutions that are identified in this section?

3.   Define the term *status*. Identify two statuses that you occupy and the institutions that they are organized around.

<u>Statuses</u>   <u>Institution</u>

a.

b.

4.   Define the term *status inconsistency*. Explain whether status inconsistency exists between the two statuses you identified above.

5.   Contrast *achieved statuses* and *ascribed statuses*. Give an example of each.

6.   Define the concept of *roles*. List some of the roles that are associated with the statuses that you identified above.

<u>Statuses</u>   <u>Roles</u>

a.

b.

7.   Define the terms *role conflict* and *role strain*. Explain whether role conflict or role strain exists between the roles you identified above.

8.   What is a *social group*?

C.   **Types of Societies.** Although several kinds of societies have existed throughout history, sociologists and anthropologists have distinguished six types based on the form of technology used in economic activities.

1.   What are the two major historical changes that have contributed to the similarity between societies today? What is the third change that, according to some sociologists, is resulting in increased similarity between many earlier forms of society?

2.   List the six principle types of society and how many years ago they emerged.

Type of Society	Emerged (years ago)
a.	
b.	
c.	
d.	

3.   *Hunting and Gathering Societies*

a.   How are hunting and gathering societies characterized?

b.   Describe the division of labor found in hunting and gathering societies.

c.   Describe the form of social structure associated with hunting and gathering societies.

4.   *Pastoral Societies*

a.   How are pastoral societies characterized?

b.   What are some of the things made possible by the production of surplus?

5. *Horticultural Societies*

    a.   Describe horticultural societies.

    b.   What are some of the roles that emerged with horticultural societies?

6. *Agricultural Societies*

    a.   Describe agricultural societies.

    b.   What is the first major technological revolution mentioned in your text? List some of the changes it brought about for the wider society.

    c.   What does it mean for a society to be *stratified*? Why does the production of surplus increase social stratification?

    d.   Define *capitalism*, and describe some of the changes brought about with the transition from feudalism to capitalism.

7. *Industrial Societies*

    a.   Describe industrial societies.

    b.   What is the second major technological revolution mentioned in your text?

c. What are some of the technological innovations that contributed to the emergence of industrial society?

d. What are some of the *institutional* changes that took place with the rise of industrial society?

8. *PostIndustrial Societies*

a. How are *industrial-capitalist societies* and *industrial-socialist societies* distinguished? What contradictions and difficulties have these forms of society faced?

b. How are postindustrial societies characterized?

c. What is the third technological revolution mentioned in your text?

d. What controversies exist among sociologists with regard to the changes brought about with the emergence of postindustrial society?

D. **Globalization: Are societies converging on a single type?**

1. What are some of the things that have contributed to globalization and to the possibility of a single type of society?

2. How has the *computer age* "shrunk the world"?

III. STUDENT ACTIVITIES

1. Modern communications technologies have made it possible to extend our definition of society beyond the notion of shared territory. What communications technologies do you use, and how have they extended your world beyond its geographical boundaries? What groups or organizations do you belong to with members from around the world?

2. Box 4.3 in your text describes how the typical American student's life is globalized. Following this example, describe how globalization is evident in your daily activities--from the moment you wake up in the morning to the time you go to bed at night. What evidence of pre-modern and modern societies is found in your activities?

IV. KEY TERMS

Listed below are some of the key terms that are introduced in Chapter 4. After you have read the chapter in your text and worked through the overview on the preceding pages, test your recall by writing the definitions of the terms in the space provided. You may check your work by referring to the *Key Terms* section at the end of the chapter in your text.

Achieved status _____

_____

Ascribed status _____

_____

Bureaucracy _____

_____

Capitalism_____

_____

Caste societies _____

_____

Contracts _____

_____

Feudalism _____

_____

Industrial society _____

_____

Productivity _____

_____

Role _____

_____

Role conflict _____

_____

Social structure _____

_____

Statuses _____

_____

Structural contradiction _____

_____

Surplus _____

_____

V.   TEST QUESTIONS

Multiple-Choice Questions
Choose the correct answer from the choices provided.

1.   Which of the following give evidence to an underlying social structure?
     a.   regularly attending classes
     b.   standing in line at the grocery store, bank, or theater
     c.   regularities in the relations between men and women
     d.   all of the above

2.   Which of the following is a social institution:
     a.   education
     b.   family
     c.   religion
     d.   all of the above

3.   A person who once held a high salaried, high prestige job and who experiences difficulty adjusting to a job with a lower salary and lower prestige is most likely experiencing:
     a.   status inconsistency
     b.   role strain
     c.   ascribed status
     d.   structural contradiction

4.   Being a student involves such behavioral expectations as, for example, being expected to attend class and to study for exams. These behavioral expectations are referred to as:
     a.   statuses
     b.   roles
     c.   institutions
     d.   norms

5. A hunting and gathering society is one that:
    a. is highly mobile.
    b. has a tribal form of social structure.
    c. has some division of labor based on gender.
    d. all of the above.

6. The production of surplus was first evidenced in:
    a. hunting and gathering societies.
    b. pastoral societies.
    c. horticultural societies.
    d. agricultural societies.

7. Industrial societies are characterized by:
    a. factory production of goods.
    b. the centralization of power.
    c. mass public education.
    d. all of the above

8. Critics argue that postindustrial society will not be a high-technology utopia, but will be characterized by:
    a. an increase in low-skill jobs that pay low wages.
    b. smaller and more flexible organizations than seen in industrial society.
    c. a decline in class-based inequalities.
    d. none of the above

9. The agricultural revolution led to:
    a. increased surplus.
    b. the stratification of society.
    c. larger populations.
    d. all of the above

10. Stratified society:
    a. is characterized by inequalities of wealth, power, and prestige.
    b. is characterized by greater equality of wealth, power, and prestige.
    c. is not seen in modern industrial society.
    d. was first evidenced in hunting and gathering societies.

True/False Questions
For each of the following statements, decide whether the statement is true or false. Write your answer in the space provided.

_____ 1. Society refers to the interacting people who share a common culture.

_____ 2. The notion of *shared territory* is a principal factor in defining a society.

_____ 3. The family is an institution that exists in every society.

_____ 4. Two of the most common bases for ascribing status are race and sex.

_____ 5. A student who has difficulty managing her time between school, work, and family responsibilities is most likely experiencing role strain.

_____ 6. Hunting and gathering societies first appeared 500,000 to 250,000 years ago.

_____ 7. A division of labor based on gender did not appear until the emergence of industrial society.

_____ 8. The predominate form of social structure associated with agricultural societies is feudalism.

_____ 9. With the emergence of industrial society, the family decreased in economic importance and increased in terms of consumption and emotional ties.

_____ 10. Socialism and capitalism are essentially the same thing.

Matching Exercise

For each of the following terms, identify the correct definition and write the appropriate letter in the space provided.

a. achieved status
b. agricultural society
c. ascribed status
d. industrial society
e. pastoral society
f. postindustrial society
g. role strain
h. social group
i. socialism
j. status inconsistency

_____ 1. an economic system characterized by the production and distribution of goods and services for the common good.

_____ 2. a status that is given for life at the moment of birth.

_____ 3. a type of society whose principal means of support is based on the factory production of goods.

_____ 4. difficulty that one experiences when contradictory expectations exist within a given role.

_____ 5. a type of society whose members domesticate wild animals and rely on them as a principal source of food and transportation.

_____ 6. a collection of people who regularly interact with one another on the basis of shared behavioral expectations and who share a sense of common identity.

_____ 7. a status that people acquire by virtue of the social positions they occupy.

_____ 8. a situation where a person occupies two or more statuses of different rank.

_____ 9. a type of society whose members cultivate crops over an extended area by means of plows, draft animals, or other technologies.

_____ 10. a type of society based on knowledge, information, and the provision of services.

Completion

Write in the word(s) that best completes each of the following statements. To check your work, you may refer to the answer key at the end of this study guide.

1. The fact that almost all college students regularly attend classes, take exams, write papers, get grades, and receive a degree provides sociologists with evidence that there is an educational _____ _____ in the United States.

2. A _____ _____ is a collection of people who regularly interact with one another on the basis of shared expectations concerning one another's behavior, and who share a sense of common identity.

3. The family, religion, education, and medicine are _____ that exist in every society.

4. Every individual occupies many _____, organized around the family, work, education, and other institutions.

5. Two major historical changes in the ways that societies provide for their sustenance are the emergence of _____ and the development of _____ _____.

6. The strong sense of commitment to one's tribe within individual Native American societies also made it difficult for different tribes to come together to resist the invasion of Europeans. This process provides an example of a _____ _____.

7. The production of _____ made it possible for pastoral societies to store food and remain in one place for a time, rather than be constantly on the move to find new food sources.

8. A _____ society is characterized by systematic inequalities in wealth, power, and prestige associated with one's social status.

9. The invention of machines to spin wool, the steam engine, and other technological innovations of the industrial age contributed to increases in worker _____.

10. Shortcomings of industrial societies based in capitalist economies led to the creation of _____, which called for the production and distribution of goods and services for the common good.

CHAPTER 5

SOCIALIZATION AND SOCIAL INTERACTION

I. LEARNING OBJECTIVES

1. To become acquainted with the sociological concepts and theories of socialization.
2. To understand when and how the process of socialization occurs.
3. To identify and become familiar with the important agents of socialization.
4. To understand how gender socialization takes place.
5. To understand the importance of social interaction to the process of socialization.
6. To consider the implications of globalization on the process of socialization.

II. CHAPTER OVERVIEW

This chapter explores the ways in which we acquire our society's beliefs and practices, and develop our sense of self.

A. **Socialization: A Lifelong Process**

   1. Define *socialization*.

   2. When does socialization occur?

B. **Nature or Nurture?** During the late nineteenth and early twentieth centuries, biological explanations of personality and human development obscured the importance of social experience in the process of socialization. In this section you will be introduced to the long-standing debate between nature and nurture in the socialization process.

   1. Briefly describe the nature-nurture debate. Where do most sociologists stand with regard to the debate?

   2. What have the accounts of deprived or isolated children revealed about the importance of social interaction in the process of socialization? Briefly describe one of the well-documented cases mentioned in your text.

C. **Theories of Socialization.** A number of important contributions have been made to our understanding of the socialization process. In this section you will become familiar with the theories of socialization that have had the greatest influence on our understanding of socialization.

1. *Behaviorism and Social Learning Theory*

    a. Define *behaviorism*. Name the two researchers with whom the origins of this approach is most closely associated. Briefly describe the focus of their research.

    b. What is social learning? How does this approach differ from the behaviorist approach to socialization?

2. *Socialization as Symbolic Interaction*

    a. What is the name of the researcher with whom the origin of this approach is most closely associated? What is the primary focus of this approach?

    b. Charles Horton Cooley developed several concepts that are useful in understanding socialization. Define the following terms and give an example or brief explanation of each.

	<u>Concept</u>	<u>Example</u>
(1)	*looking glass self*	
(2)	*primary group*	
(3)	*secondary group*	
(4)	*reference group*	

    c. What is the primary critique of behaviorism and social learning theory?

d. Define *role-taking*. Identify and describe the role-taking associated with the four principal stages of socialization developed by George Herbert Mead.

          Stages   Role-Taking

(1)

(2)

(3)

(4)

e. Mead theorized that there are two aspects of the self. What are they, and how do they relate to one another?

f. What is the primary critique of Symbolic Interactionism?

3. *Stages of Social Development*

a. Define Jean Piaget's theory of *cognitive development*. Define *egocentrism*, and explain the part it plays in a child's development.

b. According to stage theorists, what does socialization entail? What are the names of the researchers with whom this approach to socialization is most clearly associated?

c. List and describe the three principal stages of *moral development* identified by Lawrence Kohlberg.

          Stage   Description

(1)

(2)

d.   What are some of the main critiques of the stage models of socialization? What is Carol Gilligan's criticism of Kohlberg's research?

4.   *Biological Needs versus Social Constraints*

a.   Define *psychoanalysis*. What is the name of the researcher with whom this approach to socialization originated?

b.   According to Freud, when does socialization take place?

c.   According to Freud, what are the three components of the human mind? Explain the relationship between the three components.

d.   What are some of the critiques of Freud's theory of socialization?

D.   **Agents of Socialization.** Socialization occurs throughout one's lifetime and in various social contexts. List the five principal sources or *agents of socialization* mentioned in your text.

1.   *The Family and Socialization*

a.   Explain the role of the family in the process of socialization.

b.   What are some of the forces affecting the process of family socialization in the U.S.?

c.   How do family socialization practices differ based race and social class?

2.   *The School and Socialization*

a.   How has the importance of school as an agent of socialization changed since the turn of the century?

b.   Briefly explain the role of education in the process of socialization.

c.   What is school's *hidden curriculum*? Give an example.

3.   *Peers and Socialization*

a.   What are *peers*, and how do they contribute to the process of socialization?

b.   What are some of the ways in which adolescent peers socialize one another?

c.   What is *anticipatory socialization*? Give an example.

4.   *Work and Socialization*

a.   Briefly describe the social norms that are reinforced in the workplace.

b.   Explain how people might face opposing or contradictory role expectations when taking a job for the first time.

5.   *The Mass Media and Socialization*

     a.   Define *mass media*.

     b.   Give two or three examples of the ways in which television socializes children.

     c.   What have media studies concluded about the impact of media violence?

E.   **Gender Socialization.** We learn our culture's statuses, roles, norms, and rules through the various agents of socialization. We also learn culturally-defined gender roles and the norms and values associated with those roles.

    1.   List and give an example of how culturally-defined gender roles are reinforced by the agents of socialization.

          <u>Agents of Socialization</u>   <u>Example</u>

          a.

          b.

          c.

          d.

          e.

    2.   Define *heterosexuality* and *homosexuality*. Give an example illustrating how norms of sexuality are reinforced through the process of socialization.

F.   **Total Institutions and Re-socialization**

    1.   What are *total institutions*?

2. Define *re-socialization.* Describe how re-socialization is achieved in total institutions.

G. **Life-span Socialization.** Socialization is an on-going process that occurs throughout one's lifetime. While most sociological research has focused on socialization that occurs during infancy and childhood, this section will introduce you to socialization throughout the life-span.

1. Why is there a growing interest in life-span socialization in the U.S.? What is meant by the "graying" of America?

2. Erik Erikson compared childhood and adult development in different cultures. List the eight stages of development identified by Erikson and the approximate age at which they occur.

<u>Stage</u>	<u>Approximate Age</u>
a.	
b.	
c.	
d.	
e.	
f.	
g.	
h.	

3. According to Erikson, how does the individual move from one stage to the next?

4. Some sociologists emphasize the importance of culturally-influenced life experiences in the process of socialization. List and describe the four life experience groupings mentioned in your text. Identify the key experiences that occur at each period.

<u>Grouping</u>	<u>Description</u>	<u>Key Experiences</u>
a.		

b.

c.

d.

H. **Socialization and Social Interaction.** Socialization takes place primarily through social interaction, including the words, gestures, and body language that make up human communication. In this section, you will be introduced to the simple, yet important, ways in which interaction occurs and the norms that make it possible.

1. Define and give an example of the *residual norms* that govern everyday interaction.

2. Define Erving Goffman's *dramaturgical approach* to the study of social interaction.

   a. Define and give an example illustrating Goffman's notion of the *presentation of self*.

   b. What is the norm of *civil inattention*? Give an example of the norm of civil inattention.

3. What is the main insight of Harold Garfinkel's *ethnomethodology*?

4. What is the primary concern of *conversation analysis*? What has conversation analysis contributed to our understanding of social interaction?

I. **Globalization and Socialization**

1. How is our understanding of socialization globalized?

2. What are some of the issues that are raised as socialization becomes increasingly globalized?

III. STUDENT ACTIVITIES

1. List the agents of socialization that have influenced your life. Which of those is most important? How has your socialization been influenced by race, ethnic, or class issues? What forms of gender socialization can you identify?

2. Anticipatory socialization refers to the ways in which we adopt the behavior or standards of a group that we hope to emulate or join. Which groups have you aspired to join? What sorts of things have you done to prepare yourself in anticipation of becoming associated with a particular club? What are some of the things you did to prepare yourself in anticipation of becoming a student?

IV. KEY TERMS

Listed below are some of the key terms that are introduced in Chapter 5. After you have read the chapter in your text and worked through the overview on the preceding pages, test your recall by writing the definitions of the terms in the space provided. You may check your work by referring to the *Key Terms* section at the end of the chapter in your text.

egocentric _____

game stage _____

generalized other _____

hidden curriculum _____

indexicality _____

looking glass self _____

particular other _____

play stage _____

prepatory stage _____

primary groups _____

reference groups _____

re-socialization _____

role-taking _____

secondary groups _____

socialization _____

V.   TEST QUESTIONS

Multiple-Choice Questions
Choose the correct answer from the choices provided.

1.   The process of socialization is:
    a.   the way members of a society pass their culture along to one another.
    b.   a life-long process.
    c.   the process by which people develop their sense of self.
    d.   all of the above.

2.   Freud argued that:
    a.   the basic adult personality is established by age five or six.
    b.   socialization is a life-long process.
    c.   the "I" and the "me" are the basic components of the social self.
    d.   humans actively interpret the significance of words and symbols that serve as rewards and punishments.

3.   According to George Herbert Mead, children learn to take on the role of multiple others in the:
    a.   play stage.
    b.   adult stage.
    c.   game stage.
    d.   prepatory stage.

4.   Carol Gilligan's main critique of Kohlberg's stage theory of moral development is that:
    a.   it is based on the socialization and moral development of men to the exclusion of women.
    b.   it assumes that moral development is empirically testable.
    c.   it overemphasizes the importance of moral development in the process of socialization.
    d.   Carol Gilligan did not critique Kohlberg's stage theory of moral development.

5. The process of socialization in the U.S. has changed as a result of:
    a. the decline in the average number of children in a family.
    b. the increased likelihood that mothers are employed outside of the home.
    c. an increasing number of same-sex couples.
    d. all of the above.

6. Socialization often differs on the basis of:
    a. race.
    b. ethnicity.
    c. class.
    d. all of the above.

7. According to Erving Goffman, norms of civil inattention are:
    a. norms that govern how much attention one pays to another and to aspects of his or her behavior that might be embarrassing.
    b. behaviors that are found in all cultures.
    c. norms that should be taught to all children before school age to ensure civil behavior.
    d. none of the above.

8. Gender socialization occurs:
    a. in the family.
    b. through the mass media.
    c. in school.
    d. all of the above.

9. The most important agent of socialization in all societies is the:
    a. mass media.
    b. family.
    c. peer group.
    d. school.

10. Conversation analysts study:
    a. emergency telephone calls.
    b. talk and interaction during court proceedings.
    c. interruptions.
    d. all of the above.

True/False Questions
For each of the following statements, decide whether the statement is true or false. Write your answer in the space provided.

_____   1. Today most scholars no longer believe that there is a basic human nature that exists regardless of socialization.

_____ 2. Studies have shown that children deprived of significant contact with other human beings do not learn to interact or talk effectively with other human beings.

_____ 3. Sociology's main focus is on how basic needs are shaped into socially acceptable behavior.

_____ 4. Behaviorism arose during the late nineteenth century to challenge the belief that human behavior results primarily from biological instincts and drives.

_____ 5. Media studies have concluded that media violence socializes many children, teenagers, and adults into a greater acceptance of real-life violence.

_____ 6. Jean Piaget believed that cognitive development involves both social learning and biological make-up.

_____ 7. According to Lawrence Kohlberg's stage model, individuals who invoke abstract notions of right and wrong in response to a moral dilemma are at the conventional stage of moral development.

_____ 8. The family is the first source of socialization in all societies.

_____ 9. Dressing or acting in a way that will gain one's acceptance by a particular group is an example of anticipatory socialization.

_____ 10. All cultures socialize their members into unspoken norms concerning body positioning, eye contact, and the physical use of space.

Matching Exercise
For each of the following terms, identify the correct definition and write the appropriate letter in the space provided.

a.   behaviorism
b.   civil attention
c.   dramaturgical approach
d.   ethnomethodology
e.   indexicality
f.   mass media
g.   peers
h.   reality principle
i.   re-socialization
j.   total institutions

_____ 1. when members of any society renounce a substantial part of their desire for immediate pleasure in order to do the kind of work that is necessary for the society to operate smoothly.

_____ 2. people of the same age, social standing, and class.

_____ 3. an approach that emphasizes the effect of rewards and punishments on observable human behavior.

_____ 4. forms of communication that permit a one-way flow of information from a single source to a wide audience.

_____ 5. settings that isolate individuals from the rest of society in order to achieve administrative control over all aspects of their lives.

_____ 6. altering an individual's personality through total control of their environment.

_____ 7. the study of social interaction as if it were governed by norms of theatrical performance.

_____ 8. the study of common sense knowledge and procedures by which ordinary members of society make sense of their social circumstances and interactions.

_____ 9. giving off polite signals that one is aware of another person's performance.

_____ 10. the notion that the meaning of any particular action or event depends on its context.

Completion

Write in the word(s) that best completes each of the following statements. To check your work, you may refer to the answer key at the end of this study guide.

1. According to Harold Garfinkel, people's interpretation of particular events and actions serves to document the presumed existence of an underlying pattern. Garfinkel referred to this as the _____ _____ ____ _____.

2. Erving Goffman's theory that social interaction life is divided into frontstage and backstage regions is known as the _____ approach.

3. _____ is the life-long process by which people learn the values, norms, and roles of their culture, and thereby develop a sense of self.

4. George Herbert Mead believed that when children play, they practice _____, or see themselves from another person's point of view.

5.   According to Sigmund Freud, the _____ is the part of the personality that represents internalized values and norms of society.

6.   _____ ____ _____ are the groups or contexts in which the process of socialization takes place.

7.   According to Lawrence Kohlberg, the three principal stages of moral development are (in order of increasing complexity) the _____ stage, the _____ stage, and the _____ stage.

8.   The _____ refers to unspoken classroom socialization to the norms, values, and roles that occurs alongside the official school curriculum.

9.   Situations in which an individual adopts the dress or behavior of a group he or she aspires to belong to later in life are known as _____.

10.   _____ refers to the learning that occurs from observing and imitating others.

CHAPTER 6

GROUPS AND ORGANIZATIONS

I.   LEARNING OBJECTIVES

1.   To become familiar with the basic terms and concepts that organize sociological thinking about groups and organizations.
2.   To become familiar with the kinds of groups that exist and the ways in which they affect social interaction.
3.   To learn the different types of group leadership.
4.   To become familiar with the advantages and disadvantages of bureaucratic organizations, and the various alternatives to bureaucratic organizational forms.
5.   To consider how groups and organizations are influenced by increased globalization.

II.   CHAPTER OVERVIEW

Groups and organizations of one type or another are a pervasive aspect of life in modern society-- from our immediate family to such groups and organizations as schools, universities, and large, international organizations. In this chapter you are introduced to some of the main characteristics of groups and organizations, the various forms of group leadership, the advantages and disadvantages of bureaucratic organizations, and the new forms of organization emerging with increased globalization.

A.   **Social Groups.** In Chapter 4, a *social group* was defined as a collection of people who regularly interact with one another on the basis of shared expectations concerning one another's behavior, and who share a common sense of idenity. In this section, you will take a closer look at the features that characterize different types of social groups.

      1.   What are *social aggregates* and *social categories*? How are these forms distinguished from social groups?

      2.   Define and give an example of an *ingroup* and an *outgroup*. What purpose is served by identifying one's ingroup or outgroup membership?

      3.   Define and give an example of a *primary group* and a *secondary group*. According to Charles Horton Cooley, what is the basis for the term "primary" group?

a. In what ways do primary and secondary groups serve as *reference groups*, groups that provide a standard for judging one's attitudes and behaviors?

4. German sociologist Georg Simmel studied the impact of group size on people's behavior. Name and define the types of groups identified by Simmel. What is the main effect of group size on people's behavior?

Group	Definition	Main effects on behavior
a.		
b.		

5. What is the important sociological principal concerning group size and group stability first identified by Simmel? What explanations are offered for Simmel's finding?

6. Define and give an example of a *social network*.

a. Describe the form of social network in Japan's *keiretsu* and Taiwan's *guanxi*. How are these networks similar or different from networks found in the U.S.?

7. What is a *leader*? List and define the four types of leadership seen in small groups.

Leader	Definition
a.	
b.	
c.	
d.	

8. List, define, and identify the key characteristics of the two types of leadership concerned with routine group activities.

Leader	Definition	Key Characteristics

a.

b.

9.   Define the sociological notion of *power*. List the two types of power identified in your text, and identify the situations in which they are preferred or more effective.

Type of Power	When Preferred or Effective

a.

b.

10.   Sociologists have long been interested in the effects of group pressure on conformity. Group pressure, as your text points out, accounts for a great deal of conformity in all cultures.

     a.   Briefly describe the classic experiment conducted by Stanley Milgram. What was the purpose of Milgram's experiment, and what where his primary findings?

     b.   Briefly describe Philip Zimbardo's experiment. What was the purpose of his experiment, and what were his primary findings?

     c.   What is *groupthink*? Give an example from your text or from personal experience that illustrates the phenomenon of groupthink.

B.   **Organizations.** Organizations are a central feature of all societies, and their study is a central concern of sociology.

     1.   Define *organization*.

2. What did Max Weber, one of the founders of the field of organizational studies, view as the long-term trend in organizational form? What is a *formal organization*?

3. List the three types of organizations identified by Amitai Etzioni. State the principal reasons people join each type of organization, and give an example of each.

<u>Organization</u>	<u>Reasons People Join</u>	<u>Example</u>

   a.

   b.

   c.

4. How is group membership important to the development of social capital?

5. According to Max Weber, what is *bureaucratic authority*?

   a. Define Weber's notion of *ideal type* with respect to the nature of bureaucracies.

   b. List the five features identified by Weber that characterize bureaucratic organizations.

      (1)
      (2)
      (3)
      (4)
      (5)

   c. What are some of the problems or dysfunctions of bureaucracy?

6.   What is the *iron law of oligarchy*, as defined by Robert Michels? Briefly explain why, according to Michels, bureaucracy and democracy are incompatible.

7.   Define *surveillance*.

     a.   According to Gary Marx, how is the increased efficiency of surveillance in modern organizations a potential threat to individual freedom?

8.   In what ways do formal organizations construct and reinforce society's social roles? What is *occupational segregation*?

9.   In recent years, formal, bureaucratic organizations are being challenged by new, more informal, organizational forms. List and describe the key aspects of the alternative organizations mentioned in your text. Identify an organization that exemplifies each type of organization listed.

Organization	Key Aspects	Example
a.		
b.		
c.		

C.   **Globalization: Organizations that span the world.** The increase in globalization has meant an increase in organizations that are global in scope.

1.   How are the two principal types of international organization distinguished?

2.   List and describe the three types of global organizations mentioned in your text. Identify an organization that exemplifies each type.

Organization	Description	Example
a.		
b.		

c.

3. What is the *institutionalist school*, and what does it see as the main effect of globalization on institutions and organizations? Why?

III. STUDENT ACTIVITIES

1. What primary and secondary groups do you belong to? In what ways do you think the members of these social groups share expectations concerning one another's behavior and share a common identity? Is your sense of belonging to these groups distinguished by ingroup or outgroup membership?

2. Consider the organizational forms discussed in your text. How would you characterize an organization (such as your school or workplace) that you belong to? Is it a utilitarian, coercive, or normative organization? Recalling the features of an ideal type bureaucracy outlined by Max Weber, in what ways is it a bureaucratic organization? What sort of informal structure is evident in your organization?

IV. KEY TERMS

Listed below are some of the key terms that are introduced in Chapter 6. After you have read the chapter in your text and worked through the overview on the preceding pages, test your recall by writing the definitions of the terms in the space provided. You may check your work by referring to the *Key Terms* section at the end of the chapter in your text.

bureaucratic authority _____

_____

collective _____

_____

formal organization _____

_____

groupthink _____

_____

ideal-type _____

_____

ingroup _____

_____

legitimate authority _____

_____

meritocracy_____
_____

network _____
_____

outgroup_____
_____

primary group_____
_____

reference group _____
_____

secondary group_____
_____

social aggregates _____
_____

social group _____
_____

V.   TEST QUESTIONS

Multiple-Choice Questions
Choose the correct answer from the choices provided.

1.   Which is <u>not</u> an example of a social group?
   a.   a family
   b.   a college sorority
   c.   sports fans at a baseball game
   d.   roommates

2.   A group of people standing in line at a grocery store is an example of:
   a.   a social category.
   b.   a social aggregate.
   c.   a secondary group.
   d.   an outgroup.

3.   The iron law of oligarchy was proposed by:
   a.   Robert Michels.
   b.   Max Weber.
   c.   Charles Horton Cooley.
   d.   Georg Simmel.

4. Which is not an example of a secondary group?
   a. a university
   b. a school fraternity
   c. a hiking club
   d. a soccer team

5. An organized crime group is an example of:
   a. a social network.
   b. a keiretsu.
   c. a bureaucracy.
   d. none of the above.

6. Which is not a characteristic of Japanese organizations?
   a. lifetime job security
   b. quality circles
   c. increased job specialization
   d. bottom up decision-making

7. According to Max Weber, ideal-type bureaucracies are characterized by:
   a. trained incapacity.
   b. informal structure.
   c. hierarchical structure.
   d. flexibility.

8. The study of obedience to authority conducted by Stanley Milgram showed that:
   a. people will conform to orders given by someone in a position of power.
   b. people will not conform to orders by someone in a position of power if it means injuring another human being.
   c. personal power is more effective in achieving conformity than positional power.
   d. none of the above.

9. Organizations such as the Red Cross or Alcoholics Anonymous are examples of:
   a. normative organizations.
   b. coercive organizations.
   c. utilitarian organizations.
   d. collectives.

10. Which of the following is not one of the major dysfunctions of bureaucracies?
    a. goal displacement
    b. trained incapacity
    c. meritocracy
    d. incompetence

True/False Questions

For each of the following statements, decide whether the statement is true or false. Write your answer in the space provided.

_____ 1. According to Charles Horton Cooley, primary groups are the basic form of all human association.

_____ 2. According to Simmel, as groups decrease in size, their intensity decreases and their stability increases.

_____ 3. Max Weber was the first sociologist to examine in detail the characteristics of bureaucratic authority.

_____ 4. The type of power associated with the office of the U.S. President is called positional power.

_____ 5. In modern society, authority is more likely to be based on habit and custom than on reason.

_____ 6. Transactional leaders are concerned with accomplishing the groups tasks and getting members of the group to do their job.

_____ 7. Groupthink can be a hindrance to effective group decision-making.

_____ 8. Members of a secondary group have intimate ties with one another.

_____ 9. In modern bureaucratic organizations, physical surveillance is an important aspect of control.

_____ 10. All modern organizations are bureaucratic.

Matching Exercise

For each of the following terms, identify the correct definition and write the appropriate letter in the space provided.

a.   coercive organization
b.   dyad
c.   expressive leader
d.   guanxi
e.   international governmental organizations
f.   instrumental leader
g.   normative organization
h.   organization
i.   social categories

j.   transnational organizations

_____   1.   bureaucratic organizations whose operations span national boundaries, yet are centrally directed by citizens from a single country.

_____   2.   a group consisting of two persons.

_____   3.   Chinese business networks based primarily on social rather than purely economic foundations.

_____   4.   one who is concerned with accomplishing the task at hand.

_____   5.   groupings that share some common characteristic but do not necessarily interact nor identify with one another.

_____   6.   one who is concerned with the well-being of the group itself.

_____   7.   organizations established by treaties between governments for purposes of conducting business between the nations who comprise their membership.

_____   8.   a group with an identifiable membership that engages in concerted collective action to achieve a common purpose.

_____   9.   an organization in which one is forced to give unquestioned obedience to authority.

_____   10. an organization of people who join on a voluntary basis to pursue a morally worthwhile goal without expectation of material reward.

Completion
Write in the word(s) that best completes each of the following statements. To check your work, you may refer to the answer key at the end of this study guide.

1.   _____ _____ are those organizations that are rationally designed to achieve their objectives, often by means of explicit rules, regulations, and procedures.

2.   _____ groups are characterized by intense positive and negative emotional ties, whereas _____ groups are characterized by impersonality and fleeting relationships.

3.   Robert Michels argued that _____ and _____ are incompatible and that bureaucratic organizations would inevitably succumb to the iron law of _____.

4. The _____ leader instills a sense of mission or higher purpose in the members of a group, whereas _____ leaders are concerned with accomplishing a group's tasks.

5. _____ authority is power that is recognized as rightful by those over whom it is exercised.

6. A _____ consists of all the connections that link a person with other people, and through them to the persons with whom these people are connected.

7. According to Simmel, as groups _____ in size, their intensity _____, while their stability _____.

8. A _____ is a group of three persons.

9. A group that provides a standard for judging one's attitudes or behaviors is referred to as a _____ _____.

10. A group of people who are of the same age, gender, race, or income is an example of a social _____.

CHAPTER 7

DEVIANCE AND CRIME

I.   LEARNING OBJECTIVES

1.   To become familiar with the concepts and sociological theories of deviance and crime.
2.   To become familiar with the biological explanations of deviance.
3.   To understand the explanations of deviance and crime put forth by sociologists working within the functionalist, conflict, and symbolic interactionist paradigms.
4.   To become familiar with the ways in which crime is identified, measured, and controlled.
5.   To consider some of the implications of globalization on deviance and crime.

II.   CHAPTER OVERVIEW

The preceding chapters introduced you to many ways in which social life is governed by cultural norms, rules, and values. In this chapter, you will be introduced to the concepts and theories that organize sociological thinking about deviance and crime--behavior that runs counter to the prevailing social norms, rules, and values.

A.   **What Is Deviance?** In this section, you will learn how sociologists define and use the basic concepts related to deviance and crime.

   1.   Define *deviant behavior*. How do sociologists use the term "deviant"?

   2.   What is *crime*? What is the primary challenge sociologists face in attempting to explain deviance?

   3.   What is a *pluralistic* society? What are the implications of pluralism on the definition of deviance?

   4.   Define and give an example of *genocide*. How is it that genocide can be considered, under certain circumstances, perfectly normal?

B.   **Biological Explanations of Deviance.**   Today, most sociologists believe that criminal behavior is the result of socialization. Early theories of deviance, however, sought to explain deviance and criminal behavior in terms of one's biological make-up.

1.   Briefly describe Cesare Lombroso's biological theory of crime.

2.   What is *sociobiology*?

   a.   Why are twin studies especially promising in the development of sociobiological theories of crime? What have these studies revealed about biology and crime?

3.   What are the three principal weakness of sociobiological research?

   a.

   b.

   c.

C.   **Functionalist Explanations of Deviance.**   As you will recall from the preceding chapters, functionalists view society as a unitary organism made up of many different elements that serve some function in the overall performance and stability of the whole. Although it might seem odd to think that deviance has any useful function in society, in this section you will learn how functionalists view deviance and the contribution it makes to the operation of society.

1.   Emile Durkheim, the originator of functionalist theory, pioneered work in exploring the function of deviance for society. According to Durkheim, what is the primary function of deviance?

   a.   Define *anomie*. When is anomie most likely to occur?

2.   Following Durkheim, Robert K. Merton sought to explain deviance in terms of one's position in the social structure. Define Merton's notion of *structural strain*.

a. Merton's theory of deviance accounts for the various individual responses to achieving the goals of society. Chart Merton's theory of deviance below, and give an example of the individuals who are likely to fall into each category.

Individual Response	Accept/Reject Cultural Goals	Legitimacy of Means	Example
(1)			
(2)			
(3)			
(4)			
(5)			

3. Your text lists two other functionalist theories of deviance. List the theories, identify the researchers associated with each, and give a brief description of their primary argument.

Theory	Researchers	Argument
a.		
b.		

4. What is the primary critique of functionalist theory of deviance?

D. **Conflict Explanations of Deviance.** Conflict theorists argue that society is made up of different groups with conflicting interests and different standards of what is normal and what is deviant. In this section, you will become familiar with the way in which conflict theorists view deviance.

1. According to conflict theorists, how are certain acts defined as deviant for the society as a whole?
2. What is the main thesis of *structural contradiction theory*?

a. According to structural contradiction theory, which societies will have the highest level of deviance?

b. What support is there for structural contradiction theory?

3. What is the primary critique of conflict theories of deviance?

E. **Symbolic Interactionist Explanations of Deviance.** Symbolic interactionists view society as the product of social interaction among individuals. In this section, you will be introduced to the way in which normal behavior or behavior that is considered deviant is, for symbolic interactionists, interactionally achieved.

1. Describe the *labeling theory* of deviance.

a. Define and give examples of *primary deviance* and *secondary deviance*.

b. How was labeling theory applied in Howard Becker's (1963) study of marijuana use among jazz musicians?

c. Critical Thinking Box 7.2 in your text discusses Chambliss's (1973) study of the Roughnecks and Saints, two gangs of teenage boys.

(1) What did Chambliss's research reveal about the role of "visibility" and "selective perception" in labeling deviant behavior?

(2) What is "differential visibility"? What factors contributed to the differential visibility of the two gangs?

2. What is the main argument of *cultural transmission theory*?

a. Describe the theory of *differential association*. What are the names of the researchers who advanced this theory?

3. What is the primary critique of symbolic interactionist theories of deviance?

F. **Feminist Theories of Deviance.** Feminist theories of deviance and criminology begin with the observation that sociological studies of deviance are based on research on males. In this section you are introduced to feminist theories of deviance.

1. What is the fundamental question that drives feminist theories of deviance?

2. Briefly discuss the focus of early feminist theory of deviance.

3. What is the underlying argument of contemporary feminist theories of deviance?

4. What is the primary critique of feminist theory of deviance?

G. **Crime and Deviance.** You will recall that crime is a type of deviant behavior that consists of acts that are against criminal law. In this section, you will get a more detailed picture of what constitutes crime, how crime is measured, who commits crime, and how crime is controlled.

1. Describe the work of *criminologists*.

2. Define *crime*. Why do sociologists regard the definition of crime as too narrow?

3. What is the common myth about the crime rate? What is the reality?

4.	What reason is given to explain the discrepancy between crimes reported by the police and actual crime?

5.	List, define, and give examples of the four types of crime mentioned in your text?

	a.

	b.

	c.

	d.

6.	Why are crimes such as rape and assault likely to go unreported?

7.	Which groups of women are most likely to be victims of violent crime? Why?

8.	Although illegal activities are committed to some degree by nearly everyone in society, certain groups of people are more likely to be involved in criminal activity. List, define, and give an example illustrating the five different groups who are found to break the law.

	Group	Definition	Example
a.			
b.			
c.			
d.			
e.			

9.	Who is most likely to commit violent crimes such as homicide? What explanation is given for the high incidence of violent crime committed by this group?

a. What is the definition of a *gang*?

b. What does Martin Sanchez Jankowski (1991) see as the reason behind gang membership and participation?

10. Crime control in the U.S. is often perceived as the arrest and prosecution of violent criminals--those who have committed such crimes as rape or murder. According to the two studies mentioned in your text, however, what type of crimes are resulting in arrest and imprisonment?

11. In Critical Thinking Box 7.3, what explanation is given to account for the increase in arrest and imprisonment over the past 20 years?

12. Briefly explain why there is disproportionate number of young black males who are arrested and convicted of crimes.

13. What are the three primary reasons mentioned in your text to explain why people of color are more likely to be arrested and imprisoned than whites?

a.

b

c.

14. Define *incapacitation* and *rehabilitation*. What problems have been identified with respect to the effectiveness of rehabilitation?

a. Define *recidivism* and *deterrence*. Briefly describe the relationship between deterrence and recidivism.

b. What have studies concluded concerning the effectiveness of the death penalty in deterring crime?

15. The misuse of power by law enforcement officials is an ongoing topic of debate. What are some of the most common examples of misuse of power by the police or other law enforcement officials?

H. **Globalization, Crime, and Deviance.** Globalization has had wide-ranging effects on all aspects of society. In addition to raising new concerns regarding the definition of deviance as cultures come into contact with one another, globalization has made it possible for some forms of crime to prosper.

1. How has globalization had an indirect impact on crime?

2. List, describe, and give an example of two forms of crime that have prospered from globalization.

   <u>Crime</u>   <u>Description</u>   <u>Example</u>

   a.

   b.

3. What contributions can increased globalization make to ethnocentric definitions of deviance--the tendency to judge other cultures by the standards of one's own culture?

III. STUDENT ACTIVITIES

1. Deviant behavior is defined as behavior that violates social norms and values shared by people in a particular culture. As your text points out, deviant behavior can range from violating trivial norms to actions that run counter to cultural beliefs and values. Which of your behaviors or daily activities might be considered deviant outside of your circle of friends or community, or if taken to extreme?

2. In this chapter you were introduced to the different ways in which the three major sociological perspectives--functionalism, social conflict, and symbolic interactionism--think about deviance. How would each theoretical perspective

explain the case of Rodney King that was discussed in your text? Which of the three theories of deviance appeals to you? Why?

IV. KEY TERMS

Listed below are some of the key terms that are introduced in Chapter 7. After you have read the chapter in your text and worked through the overview on the preceding pages, test your recall by writing the definitions of the terms in the space provided. You may check your work by referring to the *Key Terms* section at the end of the chapter in your text.

anomie _____
_____

assault _____
_____

burglary _____
_____

crime _____
_____

deterrence _____
_____

deviant behavior _____
_____

genocide _____
_____

larceny _____
_____

pluralistic societies _____
_____

primary deviance _____
_____

recidivism _____
_____

rehabilitation _____
_____

robbery _____
_____

secondary deviance _____
_____

white collar crime _____

V. TEST QUESTIONS

Multiple-Choice Questions
Choose the correct answer from the choices provided.

1. Sociologists primarily use the term *deviant* to describe:
    a. behavior that is morally bad or wrong in a particular society.
    b. behavior that runs counter to cultural norms and values.
    c. behavior that violates criminal law.
    d. none of the above

2. According to Cesare Lombroso, deviance and criminal behavior are the result of:
    a. inherited stigmata and degeneration.
    b. early childhood socialization.
    c. anomie or conflict and confusion over the norm of society.
    d. the labels that are attached to us by other people.

3. Defining deviance is difficult because:
    a. different groups have different ideas about what is deviant and what is not.
    b. norms and values change over time.
    c. acts that are considered deviant in one social context may not be deviant in another.
    d. all of the above

4. Vagrancy and gambling are examples of:
    a. victimless crimes.
    b. interpersonal crimes.
    c. blue-collar crimes.
    d. property crimes.

5. According to your text, people of color are more likely than whites to be arrested and imprisoned because:
    a. residents of impoverished inner-city areas, where the war on drugs has been waged, are disproportionately nonwhite.
    b. police work generally focuses on poor neighborhoods.
    c. racism leads to greater arrest and imprisonment of nonwhites.
    d. all of the above.

6. According to Robert K. Merton's theory of structural strain, which of the following forms of deviance involves the acceptance of society's goals, but the rejection of legitimate means to reach those goals?
    a. ritualism
    b. innovation
    c. retreatism
    d. rebellion

7.   If you argue that deviant behavior is largely the result of associating with other persons whose behavior is deviant, you are probably following:
     a.   the theory of differential association.
     b.   labeling theory.
     c.   structural contradiction theory.
     d.   a control theory of deviance.

8.   Recidivism refers to:
     a.   resocializing criminals to non-criminal norms.
     b.   discouraging crime among the general population.
     c.   the rate at which ex-offenders are arrested for another crime after being released from jail.
     d.   none of the above

9.   Globalization has had an indirect impact on crime in the U.S. by:
     a.   creating a global economy that has resulted in the loss of jobs and increased poverty.
     b.   opening national borders, and increasing the opportunity for such criminal activities as drug trafficking and money laundering.
     c.   bringing cultures together through immigration where the behavior of the immigrant culture may be viewed as deviant by members of the dominant culture.
     d.   all of the above.

10. Functionalist theories of deviance focus on explaining deviance in terms of:
     a.   anatomical, biological, or other genetic differences.
     b.   the part it plays in defining the moral boundaries of society.
     c.   the way in which definitions of deviance reinforce the power structure of society.
     d.   the way in which deviance is learned through interaction with others.

True/False Questions
For each of the following statements, decide whether the statement is true or false. Write your answer in the space provided.

_____   1.   Deviant behavior is behavior that violates the social norms and values shared by people in a particular culture.

_____   2.   Some form of deviance is found in all societies.

_____   3.   Acts such as killing another human being and genocide are considered deviant in all societies and under all circumstances.

_____   4.   Most sociologists believe that criminal behavior is the result of socialization and other individual experiences.

_____ 5. According to functionalist theory, deviance is functional because it helps to define the moral boundaries of society.

_____ 6. Feminist theory of deviance argues that studies of deviance must direct attention away from the effects of patriarchal arrangements on delinquency.

_____ 7. According to conflict theory, groups lacking the power to have their interests defined as normal are seen as deviant.

_____ 8. Labeling theory holds that deviance is the result of the labels attached to us by others.

_____ 9. All deviant acts are criminal.

_____ 10. Most interpersonal crimes--such as murder, rape, and assault--occur between acquaintances rather than strangers.

Matching Exercise

For each of the following terms, identify the correct definition and write the appropriate letter in the space provided.

a. crime
b. deterrence
c. deviant behavior
d. genocide
e. labeling theory
f. moral boundaries
g. pluralistic societies
h. recidivism
i. victimless crime
j. white-collar crime

_____ 1. an approach that holds that deviance (like all forms of human behavior) is the result of the labels attached to us by other people.

_____ 2. a society's sense of what is normal and acceptable behavior, achieved partly by identifying certain acts as deviant and punishing them severely.

_____ 3. crime committed by people of high social status in connection with their work.

_____ 4. the impact of punishment on discouraging crime--not only on those who are punished, but on others who learn by their example.

_____ 5. societies comprised of groups with diverse and often conflicting norms and values.

_____ 6. acts prohibited by law in which those who are affected are willing and voluntary participants.

_____ 7. the rate at which ex-offenders are arrested for another criminal offense once they are released from jail.

_____ 8. the institutionalized practice of systematically killing the members of a particular racial, religious, or ethnic group.

_____ 9. behavior that violates social norms and values shared by people in a particular culture.

_____ 10. a particular form of deviance consisting of acts that violate norms and that are punishable by law.

Completion

Write in the word(s) that best completes each of the following statements. To check your work, you may refer to the answer key at the end of this study guide.

1. According to functionalist theory, a certain amount of deviance is "normal," and serves the function of defining the _____ _____ of society.

2. In Robert K. Merton's theory, structural strain is a form of anomie that occurs when a gap exists between the _____ society sets for people to achieve, and the _____ society provides for people to achieve those goals.

3. _____ _____ theory is a type of conflict theory that holds that societal strains that lead to deviance are not accidental, but rather are built into society's very structure.

4. In labeling theory, _____ deviance occurs when an activity is labeled as deviant by others, whereas _____ deviance occurs when a person labeled as deviant accepts the label as part of his or her identity.

5. According to the theory of _____ _____, the more one associates with persons whose behavior is deviant, the greater the likelihood that one's own behavior will be deviant.

6. Social scientists who specialize in the scientific study of crime are known as _____.

7.   There are two official sources of information on crime. The _____ _____ _____ consists of information provided by local police departments throughout the country, and the _____ _____ _____, which provides information based on interviews with randomly-selected Americans.

8.   _____ refers to the impact of punishment on discouraging crime--on those who are punished and on others who learn by their example.

9.   Because the U.S. is a _____ society, comprised of groups with diverse and often conflicting norms and values, it is extremely difficult to establish universally-accepted definitions of deviance.

10. The most common crimes committed in the U.S. are _____ crimes and _____ crimes.

PART III

STRUCTURES OF POWER AND INEQUALITY

CHAPTER 8

CLASS AND STRATIFICATION IN THE UNITED STATES

I.   LEARNING OBJECTIVES

1.   To understand the concept of stratification and the principal components of stratification in modern society.
2.   To become familiar with the various types of stratification systems.
3.   To explore the functionalist and social conflict theories of stratification.
4.   To become familiar with the class structure in the U.S. and the various theories of class structure.
5.   To understand what is meant by inequality and social mobility.
6.   To become familiar with the ways in which economic globalization has affected the U.S. stratification system.

II.   CHAPTER OVERVIEW

Inequality, the disparity that exists in a society, is found in every society. Social scientists use the term *stratification* to describe the systematic inequalities that exist in society.

A.   What is the definition of *social stratification*?

     1.   Define *inequality*? What are "systematic" inequalities?

     2.   List some of the factors upon which stratification is based?

B.   **Stratification in Modern Societies: Class, Status, and Power.** Chapter 4 introduced you to the principal types of society that have existed throughout history. In this section, you will become familiar with the way in which societies are stratified on the basis of class, status, and power.

     1.   Briefly explain why stratification became more pronounced with the move to agricultural societies?

     2.   Describe the stratification system that emerged with the industrial revolution.

3. List and define the three interrelated aspects of stratification as developed by Max Weber.

        Aspect   Definition

a.

b.

c.

4. What are the three components of social class?

   a. List, define, and give an example of the jobs found in the three types of occupation classifications.

        Occupation   Definition   Example

      (1)

      (2)

      (3)

   b. Define *net financial asset*. Compare the median wealth for the top-earning fifth of American households to the median wealth for the bottom fifth?

   c. A wealth gap persists between African Americans and whites. What factors account for this disparity in wealth?

   d. Briefly explain and give an example illustrating how wealth can be measured by differences in privilege.

   e. Which occupations are classified as high status or prestige? Which occupations are ranked as low prestige? On what basis is this distinction made?

f.   Describe the "shape" of power stratification in the U.S.

g.   List and define the three theories of power presented in your text.

Theory of Power	Definition

(1)

(2)

(3)

C.   Changes in Stratification: Caste, Class, or Classless Society?

1.   What does it mean to say that stratification systems can be "open" or "closed"?

2.   List, define, and provide an example of the three principal types of stratification systems mentioned in your text. State whether they are open or closed systems.

System	Definition	Example	Open or Closed

a.

b.

c.

3.   Contrast the way in which class membership is determined in caste and class stratification systems.

4.   Why has caste stratification systems given way to class stratification systems?

5.   What did Marx believe to be necessary for class stratification systems to exist?

a. According to Marx, why were hunting and gathering societies classless?

b. What did Marx predict about the transition from industrial capitalism to communism?

D. **Why does stratification exist?** The fact that some societies have made direct efforts to reduce inequality raises the question of why stratification exists. There are two principal and competing approaches that seek to answer this question.

1. Functionalist theories seek to identify and explain the ways in which stratification is functional for the operation of society as a whole.

   a. Basing their work on the writings of Emile Durkheim, Kingsley Davis and Wilbert Moore developed a functionalist theory of inequality. What is the main thesis of Davis and Moore's theory?

   b. What are the implications of the Davis-Moore theory for public policy?

   c. What are two primary critiques of the Davis-Moore theory?

2. Based on the writings of Karl Marx, social conflict theories hold that conflict is central to all forms of society. In this view, stratification reflects the struggle between different classes.

   a. What are the two broad classes distinguished by Marx?

   b. Briefly characterize the conflict between the two classes.

   c. According to Marx, workers would resist the move toward capitalism by developing *class consciousness*. What is class consciousness?

d.   According to Marx, what would it take to bring about a conflict-free, classless society?

e.   On what basis did Max Weber disagree with Marx?

f.   What alternative explanation did Weber give for social conflict?

g.   What is the primary critique of conflict theories of stratification?

E.   **A Picture of the U.S. Class Structure.** Class structures differ between societies. In this section you are introduced to the U.S. class structure.

1.   List the class and subclass categories of U.S. class structure below. Briefly describe the occupational make-up of each class or subclass and the percent of the total population represented in each.

         <u>Class</u>   <u>Description</u>   <u>% of Population</u>

         a.

         b.
            (1)

            (2)

         c.

2.   Define *urban underclass*.

         a.   Why, according to Wilson, does the U.S. have an underclass?

b. Describe the make-up of the urban underclass?

c. What social forces have contributed to the emergence of the underclass?

3. Wilson's theory of the underclass in America has come under much scrutiny. What is the main critique of Wilson's theory?

F. **Theories of Class Structure.** In this section you are introduced to two theories that attempt to explain why classes exist.

1. What is the main thesis of Erik Ohlin Wright's theory of class location and power?

a. According to Wright, the stratification system of industrial society is made up of seven classes--the first four of which are directly involved in large-scale economic relations. List the classes below, describe their make-up, and identify their relationship to capitalist enterprises.

Class	Description	Relationship
(1)		
(2)		
(3)		
(4)		
(5)		
(6)		
(7)		

b. Define *contradictory class location.* Which of the groups in Wright's class structure occupy contradictory class locations?

2.   Define *professional-managerial class*. What is the main thesis of Ehrenreich's theory of the professional-managerial class?

   a.   What are the three classes that make up the Ehrenreich class structure?

   b.   What percent of the American population makes up the professional-managerial class?

   c.   Why is the professional-managerial class thought to be a contradictory class location?

G.   **Inequality in the United States.** The study of social inequality is one of the most important areas of sociology. In this section, you are introduced to what sociological research has revealed about inequality in the U.S.

   1.   Although the average income in the U.S. has increased, not all Americans have experienced economic gains. Inequalities in wealth based on gender, race, and ethnicity continue to exist.

      a.   Table 8.2 in your text shows the median household income and poverty rates by race. What percent of the median white household income are the median incomes of African American households and Hispanic households?

      b.   Figure 8.3 in your text compares the concentration of income in the U.S. with other industrialized nations. According to the information provided, which nation has the highest ratio of inequality (average income of the wealthiest fifth of all households to the poorest fifth)? Which two countries have the lowest ratios of inequality?

c. Until the early 1970s, the average American male worker's income could be expected to increase continuously until retirement. Describe the trend in the average American male worker's earning power since the 1970s.

d. According to the U.S. government, how is "poverty level" defined? Using this definition, how many Americans are living below the "poverty line"?

e. Who are the *working poor*?

f. What is meant by the *feminization of poverty*? What factors have contributed to the feminization of poverty?

g. In the mid to late 1960s, President Johnson's "War on Poverty" helped to reduce the number of Americans living in poverty. Why has poverty continued to climb since the early 1970s?

2. Define *homelessness*.

a. Who are today's homeless as compared to the homeless of a generation ago?

b. Although it is difficult to know how many homeless people there really are, what are the most widely accepted figures on the number of homeless in America?

c. What are some of the *personal causes* of homelessness? What is the primary critique of this approach to understanding homelessness?

d. What are some of the *societal causes* of homelessness?

e. What is the sociological explanation for homelessness?

f. Who is most at risk of becoming homeless?

3. Briefly explain why inequality is growing in the U.S.

H. **Social Mobility: Who gets ahead.** In this section you are introduced to the concepts that help organize sociological thinking about social mobility.

1. Define *social mobility*.

2. Define the two types of social mobility that distinguish the period of time over which mobility occurs: *inter-generational* and *intra-generational mobility*

a.

b.

3. What is *structural mobility*? Give an example that illustrates structural mobility.

4. Define *positional mobility*. Briefly explain Blau and Duncan's (1967) findings concerning men's positional mobility.

5. What is the positional mobility pattern for women? African Americans? Latinos?

6. Define *cultural capital*. What aspects of middle class home life in the U.S. contribute to one's cultural capital?

7.   What part does *individual effort* play in one's social mobility?

I.   **Globalization and Stratification in the United States: A Summary**

1.   What are the two primary impacts of economic globalization on stratification in the U.S.?

a.

b.

2.   Recalling Box 8.3 in your text, what argument does labor specialist Richard Rothstein make about wage differentials between the U.S. and other countries?

III.   **STUDENT ACTIVITIES**

1.   In this chapter you have been introduced to class and stratification in the U.S. Using the definitions in your text as a guide, which class do you belong to? What characteristics identify you as a member of this class? Describe the social mobility that you or others in your family have experienced? Describe any inter-generational mobility that has occurred in your family.

2.   Functionalist theories of stratification emphasize the ways in which stratification strengthens the society as a whole; whereas social conflict theories argue that stratification results from conflict between the two competing classes. Which of these theories of stratification appeals to you? Do you agree with Davis and Moore that inequality exists to "insure that the most important positions are conscientiously filled by the most qualified persons"? If so, how would you respond to the criticism that the difference in rewards between positions is not impartially allocated?

IV.   **KEY TERMS**

Listed below are some of the key terms that are introduced in Chapter 8. After you have read the chapter in your text and worked through the overview on the preceding pages, test your recall by writing the definitions of the terms in the space provided. You may check your work by referring to the *Key Terms* section at the end of the chapter in your text.

affordability gap _____

_____

blue collar work _____

_____

class consciousness _____

_____

class dominance _____

_____

contradictory class location _____

_____

deinstitutionalization _____

_____

endogamy _____

_____

feminization of poverty _____

_____

inequality _____

_____

Kuznets curve_____

_____

pink collar work _____

_____

ritual pollution _____

_____

social stratification _____

_____

structural mobility _____

_____

V.   TEST QUESTIONS

Multiple-Choice Questions
Choose the correct answer from the choices provided.

1.   The numerically largest strata in industrial societies is the:
    a.   upper class.
    b.   middle class.
    c.   working class.
    d.   lower class.

2.   According to Max Weber, stratification consists of three interrelated aspects:
       a.   class, status, power
       b.   class, social mobility, power
       c.   power, net financial assets, cultural capital
       d.   none of the above

3.   Sociologists have identified three important components of one's social class position.
       They are:
       a.   gender, race, ethnicity
       b.   cultural capital, net financial assets, social mobility
       c.   occupation, income, wealth
       d.   occupation, income, power

4.   The Kuznets curve hypothesizes that inequality:
       a.   increases during the early stages of capitalist development, and gradually decreases
              thereafter.
       b.   decreases during the early stages of capitalist development, and gradually increases
              thereafter.
       c.   increases during the early stages of capitalist development, and continues to
              increase at a steady rate.
       d.   increases during the early stages of capitalist development, declines, and eventually
              stabilizes at a low level.

5.   According to the Davis-Moore theory, inequality:
       a.   insures that the most important positions are filled by the most qualified persons.
       b.   is dysfunctional in all societies.
       c.   reflects the winners and losers in the struggle for supremacy between different
              classes.
       d.   reflects the impact of globalization on the U.S. economy.

6.   Movement through the stratification system that occurs across generations is referred to
       as:
       a.   lateral mobility.
       b.   vertical mobility.
       c.   inter-generational mobility.
       d.   intra-generational mobility.

7.   In caste societies, caste membership is based on:
       a.   what one does.
       b.   economic position.
       c.   family background.
       d.   ascription.

8. Workers who have some of the power of the bourgeoisie, yet, like members of the working class, are in many ways denied such power are in what Wright terms:
   a. the underclass.
   b. a contradictory class location.
   c. the professional-managerial class.
   d. class dominance.

9. Endogamy refers to:
   a. the acquisition of one's position in the stratification system on the basis of heredity.
   b. a prohibition against marrying or having sexual relations with persons outside of one's social group.
   c. the difference between what poor people pay for housing and what they can afford to pay.
   d. the verbal skills, knowledge base, and ways of thinking that help one get ahead.

10. Using the U.S. government's definition of the "poverty level," approximately how many Americans are currently living in poverty?
    a. 6 million
    b. 12 million
    c. 24 million
    d. 38 million

True/False Questions
For each of the following statements, decide whether the statement is true or false. Write your answer in the space provided.

_____ 1. All societies in the modern world are stratified on the basis of wealth, power, and prestige.

_____ 2. There are no caste societies in existence in today's modern world.

_____ 3. According to Karl Marx, communism would eventually emerge out of capitalism.

_____ 4. Research has shown that men and women are equally able to achieve upward mobility.

_____ 5. Family background has the strongest effect on one's own life chances.

_____ 6. The feminization of poverty refers to the increase in the number of poor who are women.

_____ 7. Movement through the stratification system that results from individual effort or luck is referred to as structural mobility.

_____ 8. African Americans and Latinos now experience the same level of upward mobility as whites.

_____ 9. Studies show that throughout the twentieth century, downward mobility has been more common than upward mobility.

_____ 10. In modern industrial society, power is distributed equally among all members of the population.

Matching Exercise

For each of the following terms, identify the correct definition and write the appropriate letter in the space provided.

a. caste societies
b. class
c. downward mobility
d. inter-generational mobility
e. net financial assets
f. occupation
g. positional mobility
h. power
i underclass
j. working poor

_____ 1. movement through the stratification system that results in a decrease in occupational status.

_____ 2. one's relationship to governmental and other political institutions, manifested in the ability to mobilize resources and achieve a goal despite the resistance of others.

_____ 3. a caste-like class that is beneath the class system in that it even lacks access to the lower parts of the working class.

_____ 4. societies in which the strata are closed to movement, so that one must remain throughout one's life in the stratum of one's birth.

_____ 5. the value of everything one owns, minus the value of everything one owes.

_____ 6. movement through the stratification systems that results from individual effort, accomplishments, or luck, rather than changes in the occupational structure.

_____ 7. people whose earnings are insufficient to lift them above poverty.

_____ 8. movement through the stratification system that occurs across generations.

_____ 9. one's location in a society's economic system, resulting in differences in the nature of work, income, and wealth.

_____ 10. paid employment.

Completion
Write in the word(s) that best completes each of the following statements. To check your work, you may refer to the answer key at the end of this study guide.

1. _____ refers to the value of everything one owns, whereas _____ refers to the amount of money a person or household earns in a given period of time.

2. _____ refers to the growing number of homeless mentally ill people on the streets and in shelters that has resulted from the closure of many public mental hospitals.

3 _____ _____ is a theory that holds that power is concentrated in the hands of a relatively small number of individuals who comprise the upper class power elite.

4. A home life that emphasizes scholastic achievement and the development of a child's verbal skills is increasing that child's _____ _____ .

5. Being the first person in a working class family to earn a college degree to become a lawyer is an example of _____ mobility.

6. The wealthiest Americans--the heads of major corporations, movie and television stars, professional athletes--are considered to be members of the _____ class.

7. In South Africa, apartheid--the rigid separation of the population based on race--is an example of a _____ stratification system.

8. _____ _____ refers to the systematic inequalities of wealth, power, and prestige that result from one's social rank.

9. Erik Ohlin Wright proposed the notion of _____ _____ _____ to describe the position of workers whose work partly gives them the power of the bourgeoise class, yet at the same time, like members of the working class, they are often denied such power.

10. _____ _____ refers to the movement of individuals or groups through the stratification system, particularly as resulting from changes in occupation, wealth, or income.

CHAPTER 9

GLOBAL INEQUALITY

I.   LEARNING OBJECTIVES

1.   To become familiar with global stratification and the way in which the nations of the world are economically stratified.
2.   To become familiar with the concepts and sociological theories that attempt to explain global inequality.
3.   To become familar with the rapidly growing economies of the world and the implications for global inequality.

II.   CHAPTER OVERVIEW

In Chapter 8 you were introduced to the issues surrounding inequality and stratification in the United States. In this chapter, you are introduced to global inequality and the ways in which the nations of the world can be divided into economic stratum.

A.   **Wealth, Poverty, and Global Stratification**

   1.   In Chapter 8, *social stratification* was defined as the systematic inequalities in wealth, power, and prestige that results from one's social rank. Restate this definition as it applies to the world as a whole.

   2.   Prior to the 1990s, global stratification was characterized in terms of "three worlds." List and define these three zones, and name two or three nations that represent each world.

World	Definition	Nations
a.		
b.		
c.		

   3.   Why is the "three world" distinction between nations no longer useful?

4. One way to stratify countries is in terms of the wealth of their average citizen. Define *Gross National Product*, and explain how this measure is calculated.

    a. Why is GNP sometimes a misleading measure by which to stratify countries?

    b. What other measures are used to stratify countries?

5. Table 9.1 in your text compares low, middle, and high income nations on a number of measures.

    a. Which strata do most nations fall within?

    b. Which strata contains the largest population? The smallest population?

    c. Which strata has the highest birth rate? What effect is this having on this strata of nations?

    d. What does poverty mean in a global context?

    e. Which strata consumes the most energy per person? Which strata has had the greatest increase in per person energy consumption between 1965 and 1990.

    f. Contrast the average life expectancy at birth of people in high-income nations and low-income nations. What is the major cause of the difference?

6. List some of the social conditions that shape the impact of "natural" disasters on low and high income nations.

Low Income Countries	High Income Countries
_____	_____
_____	_____
_____	_____
_____	_____

7. What are some of the social causes of famine and starvation in the world today?

8. Your text points out that while food production in the world continues to increase, world hunger continues to grow. What explanation is offered for this?

B. **Theories of Global Inequality.** In this section you are introduced to the three kinds of theories that attempt to account for global inequality.

1. What is the fundamental assumption behind *market-oriented theories*?

    a. W. W. Rostow's theory of *modernization* is one type of market-oriented theory. According to Rostow, what do barriers to development in low-income countries result from? Give an example that illustrates Rostow's argument.

    b. What does it mean for a country to be *fatalistic*?

    c. According to Rostow, economic growth goes through several stages. List and characterize the key aspects of each stage below.

Stage	Key aspects
(1)	
(2)	
(3)	
(4)	

    d. What evidence is offered to support Rostow's claim that the adoption of modern, capitalist institutions leads to economic development?

2. What is the weakness of market-oriented theories?

110

3.   Briefly explain Marx's belief concerning inequality between countries. List the three economic strategies that support this view.

    a.

    b.

    c.

4.   Define *colonialism*.

5.   During the 1960s, many theorists began to question the market-oriented explanations of global stratification. What was their main critique?

6.   What is the fundamental assumption behind *dependency theory*?

    a.   What, according to this theory, does the dependency of low income nations on wealthy nations result from?

    b.   What is the primary critique of dependency theory? Give an example from your text to illustrate this critique.

7.   What is the fundamental assumption behind *world systems theory*?

    a.   According to world system theory, the global economic system can be divided into three zones.   List, define, and describe the relationship between the three zones below.

	Zone	Definition	Relationship
(1)			
(2)			
(3)			

b.   What is *hegemonic power*? How does such power fit into world system theory?

8.   Related to Wallerstein's theory is a new theory termed the *New International Division of Labor (NIDL)*. What is the fundamental assumption of the NIDL?

a.   How does the global division of labor reinforce inequality between nations?

9.   What is a *commodity chain*. What does a commodity chain network consist of?

a.   How does the commodity chain approach differ from other world systems theories in terms of its core and peripheral components?

10.   What are some of the primary criticisms of the various forms of world system theory?

C.   **The Newly Industrializing Countries (NICS)**

1.   What are *newly industrializing countries (NICS)*? Which countries constitute make-up the East Asian *newly industrializing countries*?

2. What do the economic growth statistics reveal about what has happened in the East Asian region over the last quarter century?

3. What are some of the historical factors that have contributed to the success of the East Asian NICs?

4. What cultural factors have contributed to the NICs?

5. How have the governments of East Asian NICs helped to shape their economic growth?

6. What costs are associated with the economic growth of East Asian NICs?

D. **Globalization: The Future of Economic Inequality.** Sociologists are not only interested in the issues surrounding global stratification, but also in understanding the relationships that give rise to economic growth and decline.

1. What is the principal challenge to a single, global capitalist economy?

2. Why does the People's Republic of China play such an important role in the future of the global economy?

3. Your text mentions two possible outcomes that the changes taking place in China might have for the future of global inequality. What are they?

    a.

    b.

III. STUDENT ACTIVITIES

1. Which theory of global inequality appeals to you? Why is this theory more appealing than the others? What solutions might each theory propose to confront global inequality? Consider, for example, how each theory might propose to deal with famine and starvation, health-related issues that affect birth and death rates, or illiteracy.

2. The statistics presented in your text concerning global starvation, famine, and the impact of "natural" disasters are startling, yet social conditions continue to exist in low-income nations that prevent them from averting the brunt of such disasters. What solutions would you propose?

IV. KEY TERMS

Listed below are some of the key terms that are introduced in Chapter 9. After you have read the chapter in your text and worked through the overview on the preceding pages, test your recall by writing the definitions of the terms in the space provided. You may check your work by referring to the *Key Terms* section at the end of the chapter in your text.

colonialism _____

_____

commodity chain _____

_____

core countries _____

_____

first world _____

_____

gross national product _____

_____

modernization theory _____

_____

newly-industrializing countries _____

_____

peripheral countries _____

_____

second world _____

_____

third world _____

_____

V.   TEST QUESTIONS

Multiple-Choice Questions
Choose the correct answer from the choices provided.

1.   The "three world" distinction is not as useful as it once was in describing the nations of the world because:
    a.   the "second world" ended with the dissolution of the Soviet Union and its Eastern European allies.
    b.   it masks many of the differences between the nations included in the "third world" strata.
    c.   the first, second, and third world ranking reflects a value judgment on the countries in each strata.
    d.   all of the above

2.   Although death rates are similar between the low, middle, and high income strata nations, the birth rate for low nations is twice that of high income nations. As a consequence:
    a.   the population of high income nations is growing three times faster than low income nations.
    b.   the population of low income nations is growing three times faster than high income nations.
    c.   the populations of low and high income nations are growing at the same rate.
    d.   none of the above.

3.   Which of the following statements are true of global poverty?
    a.   Two-thirds of the world's poor are under the age of fifteen.
    b.   The poorest households tend to be female-headed throughout the world.
    c.   Approximately 325 million impoverished persons live in sub-Saharan Africa.
    d.   All of the above are true of global poverty.

4.   Market-oriented theories of global inequality argue that:
    a.   unrestricted capitalism is the best possible avenue to economic growth.
    b.   capitalism is the cause of inequality between nations.
    c.   the poverty of low income nations is the result of their dependence on wealthy nations.
    d.   the division of labor between industrial societies relegates low income nations to the role of providing cheap labor for firms based in high income nations.

5.   The number of people in the world living in poverty is approximately:
    a.   5.5 million.
    b.   25 million.
    c.   1.2 billion.
    d.   3.5 billion.

6. According to the per-person gross national product, the average income in high income nations is:
   a. 3 times that of low income nations.
   b. 25 times that of low income nations.
   c. 45 times that of low income nations.
   d. 61 times that of low income nations.

7. That idea that low income countries are fatalistic--having value systems that view hardship and suffering as unavoidable features of daily life--is proposed by which theory of global inequality?
   a. dependency theory
   b. modernization theory
   c. world systems theory
   d. dependent development theory

8. According to the world systems perspective, the network of labor and production processes whose end result is a finished product comprise the:
   a. semiperipheral activities.
   b. peripheral activities.
   c. commodity chain.
   d. interstate system.

9. Which of the following is not one of the factors sociologists have identified that explain the success of the East Asian NICs?
   a. East Asian NICs were not subject to economic, social, and political exploitation by industrial powers.
   b. Cultural homogeneity and an emphasis on the importance of education and hard work.
   c. Governmental support of economic and social programs that enable economic development.
   d. Trade unions and other organizations that work to ensure safe working conditions and competitive wages for workers.

10. Research has shown that while most everyone attends high school in high income nations, attendance in low income nations is only:
    a. 18 percent.
    b. 30 percent.
    c. 38 percent.
    d. 42 percent.

True/False Questions
For each of the following statements, decide whether the statement is true or false. Write your answer in the space provided.

_____ 1. The gap between rich and poor countries is growing.

_____ 2. Throughout the world, the poorest households tend to be female-headed.

_____ 3. The difference in energy consumption between low and high income nations has declined primarily because wealthier nations are conserving energy and consuming less.

_____ 4. According to W.W. Rostow, capitalist institutions are the key to economic growth for low income countries.

_____ 5. Marxist theories tend to view global inequality as the result of high income nations exploiting low income nations.

_____ 6. Modernization and other market-oriented theories originated in low income nations in the mid-1980s.

_____ 7. Wallerstein's version of world system theories emphasize the relations between core, periphery, and semi-periphery in the world economic system.

_____ 8. According to new international division of labor theorists, profitable high-skill labor activities are distributed among low income nations to improve their chances of economic success.

_____ 9. Although prestige is an important factor in determining the social rank of an individual or group, it does not apply at the global level since there are no common global cultural norms.

_____ 10. The per-person gross national product (GNP) is a measure of a country's yearly output of wealth, per-person.

Matching Exercise
For each of the following terms, identify the correct definition and write the appropriate letter in the space provided.

a. core activities
b. core countries
c. dependency theory
d. market-oriented theories
e. modernization theory

f.   new international division of labor theory
g.   newly industrializing countries
h.   peripheral activities
i   semi-peripheral countries
j.   world systems theory

_____   1.   a theory of economic development that argues that low-income nations can become modern by "taking-off" into self-sustained economic growth only if they overcome fatalistic value systems.

_____   2.   according to commodity chain theory, these are the economic activities where profits are made.

_____   3.   a theory of economic development that argues that the division of labor that characterizes industrial societies relegates low income nations to the role of providing cheap labor.

_____   4.   a Marxist theory of economic development that argues that the poverty of low income nations is the immediate consequence of their exploitation by wealth nations.

_____   5.   theories about economic development that assume that the best possible economic consequences will result if individuals are free to make their own economic decisions, free of governmental constraint.

_____   6.   according to commodity chain theory, these are the economic activities from which profits are taken.

_____   7.   rapidly growing economies of the world.

_____   8.   a theory that argues that the world capitalist economic system must be understood as a single unit, rather than in terms of individual countries.

_____   9.   according to world systems theory, these are the countries that occupy an intermediate position in the global capitalist economy.

_____   10.   according to world systems theory, these are the most advanced industrial nations.

Completion
Write in the word(s) that best completes each of the following statements. To check your work, you may refer to the answer key at the end of this study guide.

1.   _____ theories of global inequality claim that cultural and institutional barriers to development explain the poverty of low income nations.

2.	_____ theory is a type of market-oriented theory that argues that low income nations can become modern by "taking-off" into self-sustained economic growth only if they overcome fatalistic value systems.

3.	According to modernization theory, the _____ stage of economic growth is characterized by low rates of savings, the lack of a work ethic, and a fatalistic value system.

4.	Dividing the total wealth of a country by its total population yields the _____ _____ _____.

5.	_____ theories argue that global capitalism has locked the poor countries of the world into a downward spiral of exploitation and poverty.

6.	_____ is a system under which powerful countries establish, for their own profit, rule over weaker peoples or countries.

7.	According to Wallerstein's version of world systems theory, the world economic system can be divided into three levels: _____, _____, and _____.

8.	_____ _____ _____ _____ theorists argue that the drive to find ever-cheaper labor has led transnational corporations to locate their factories wherever the cheapest labor can be found.

9.	The _____ _____ approach suggests that economic activities can be broken down into two groups: _____ activities and _____ activities.

10.	The effect of "natural" disasters on countries have much to do with the _____ _____ that characterize their populations.

CHAPTER 10

RACE AND ETHNICITY

I.   LEARNING OBJECTIVES

1.   To become familiar with the sociological concepts of race and ethnicity.
2.   To understand how the concepts of race and ethnicity are socially constructed.
3.   To understand how race and ethnicity are linked to prejudice, discrimination, and inequality.
4.   To become familiar with the racial and ethnic diversity in the U.S.
5.   To understand the effect of globalization on race and ethnic relations.

II.   CHAPTER OVERVIEW

This chapter explores the racial and ethnic diversity in the U.S. and the problems confronting the different minority groups that make up American society.

A.   **Introduction: Many societies, separate and equal?**

1.   Chapter 10 begins by introducing you to a series of studies of race and race relations in the United States. On the chart below, state the name of the researcher or commission who conducted each study, when they were conducted, and their primary findings.

Conducted by	When Conducted	Findings
a.		
b.		
c.		
d.		

B.   **The Social Construction of Race and Ethnicity.** In this section you will be introduced to the concepts of race and ethnicity and some of the sources of such distinctions.

1.   This section begins with an observation made by W.I. Thomas, one of the founders of sociology. State Thomas's theorem below, and briefly explain what it means with respect to race and ethnicity.

2.   Define *race*.

        a.   What factors are often used to classify persons by race.

        b.   What does it mean to say that variations <u>within</u> any racial category are greater than the variations <u>between</u> racial categories?

        c.   How do sociologists view classification based on biological characteristics?

        d.   What has archeological research contributed to our understanding of race?

        e.   How are the concepts of race socially constructed within a culture?

3.   Define *ethnicity*.

        a.   List some of the different ethnic groups mentioned in your text.

        b.   On what basis are ethnic groups distinguished?

        c.   What is the sociological significance of placing people in a particular racial or ethnic group?

4.   Define *minority group*.

a. According to most sociologists, what distinguishes a group as a minority? Give an example illustrating the distinction.

C. **Relations Between Dominant and Minority Groups.** In this section you are introduced to the three ways in which sociologists explain the relations between dominant and minority groups in the U.S.

1. Define *assimilation*, and explain the 'melting pot' imagery of assimilation.

a. Define *acculturation*, and briefly explain how it can shape the experience of minority groups.

2. Define *segregation*.

a. Is segregation still in existence in the U.S.? Briefly explain.

b. What is the impact of segregation on minority groups?

3. Define *cultural pluralism*.

a. How does the cultural pluralism model view segregation?

b. What is an *ethnic economic enclave*? Give an example.

D.   **Prejudice**

1.   Define *prejudice.*

    a.   Two forms of prejudice are presented in your text: *racism* and *stereotyping.* Define and give examples illustrating each form.

    b.   Racism is found in most cultures. What have national public opinion polls revealed about racism in the U.S.? What questions arise concerning the results of such polls?

    c.   Briefly describe the common stereotypes regarding the success of blacks in athletics. What purpose do such stereotypes serve for members of the dominant culture?

    d.   Stereotypes can be both negative and positive. What are the stereotypes regarding Asian Americans?

        (1)   Define *model minority,* and explain how such positive stereotypes can be used against a minority.

    e.   Define and give an example illustrating *scapegoating.*

E.   **Discrimination**

1.   Define *discrimination.*

    a.   What effect did Civil Rights movements of the 1950s and 1960s have on discrimination in the U.S.?

b.   Although progress has been made, racial and ethnic discrimination continues to be a problem in the U.S. Define and give examples of the following forms of discrimination.

                                                    Definition   Example

    (1)   *Redlining*

    (2)   *Institutional discrimination*

2.   Title VII of the Civil Rights Act of 1964 instituted *affirmative action* laws. What is affirmative action, and briefly explain its purpose.

    a.   How are affirmative action laws currently interpreted with regard to hiring?

    b.   Briefly describe how support for affirmative action differs between African Americans and whites.

    c.   What is 'reverse discrimination', and what has research shown concerning the effects of affirmative action?

3.   What impact has affirmative action had on discrimination in the U.S.?

F.   **Racial and Ethnic Groups in the United States.** In this section, you are introduced to racial and ethnic diversity in the United States and the unique histories of different racial and ethnic groups.

1.   Your text makes an important distinction between racial and ethnic groups who became a part of American society by choice and those who had little choice in the matter. Many people came to America as *indentured servants* or as slaves. Define *indentured servants*. Who were they?

2.   When were slaves first brought from Africa? What proportion of the early American population was of African origin?

3.   Table 10.2 in your text summarizes current and projected changes in minority population of the U.S.

     a.   African Americans made up what percent of the population in 1992? What is the projected percent for the year 2000? What is the anticipated percent increase between 1992 and 2050?

     b.   Latinos made up what percent of the population in 1992? What is the projected percent for the year 2000? What is the anticipated percent increase between 1992 and 2050?

     c.   Asian Americans made up what percent of the population in 1992? What is the projected percent for the year 2000? What is the anticipated percent increase between 1992 and 2050?

     d.   Native Americans made up what percent of the population in 1992? What is the projected percent for the year 2000? What is the anticipated percent increase between 1992 and 2050?

     e.   Which group is anticipated to have the greatest increase in representation among the American population between 1992 and 2050?

4.   The arrival of European settlers greatly impacted the lives of the indigenous peoples of North America. What are some of the factors that contributed to the defeat of Native American societies?

     a.   What are *reservations*, and what purpose did they serve during the nineteenth century?

b.   Describe the living standard of the Native American population in the U.S. today.

5.   Briefly describe the historical events surrounding slavery in America.

    a.   What event brought an end to slavery?

    b.   Describe the impact of the "Jim Crow" laws on the African American population?

    c.   Describe the event that played a key role in bringing about the Civil Rights movement of the 1950s.

    d.   Describe the living standard of the African American population in the U.S. today.

    e.   What income, educational, and political gains have African Americans made since the 1960s?

6.   What cultures are included in the category "Latinos"?

    a.   What historical event led to the early introduction of Mexicans to the U.S.?

    b.   Describe the living standard of the Mexican American population.

c.   Describe the introduction of Puerto Ricans to the U.S. and their contemporary living standard.

d.   How was the introduction of Cuban Americans to the U.S. different than that of other Latino groups?

e.   Describe the living standard of Cuban Americans in the U.S. today. What factors make their experience different than the experience of the other Latino groups?

7.   Describe the events leading up to the introduction of Asian peoples to the U.S.

a.   Describe the experience of the Asian American population during WWII.

b.   What factors have contributed to the economic success of many Asian Americans?

8.   Who are the White Ethnic Americans?

a.   What factors made acculturation easier for white ethnic immigrants than, for example, Latinos or Asians?

9.   Who are the New Immigrants?

a.   What is the primary reason these groups are immigrating to the U.S.?

b. How has globalization contributed to the increase in immigration to the U.S.?

G. **Globalization, Race, and Ethnicity.** Increased contact between racial and ethnic groups can lead to increased strife or to an appreciation of cultural differences.

1. Explain how increased contact between racial and ethnic groups lead to increased tension between groups.

   a. Explain how acts of racial or ethnic violence can result from increased globalization. Give an example illustrating how globalization has contributed to these conflicts.

2. Explain how globalization can contribute to racial and ethnic harmony.

   a. What part does global media play in decreasing racial and ethnic strife?

   b. Why is it so difficult to solve the world's racial and ethnic problems?

III. STUDENT ACTIVITIES

1. Do you consider yourself to belong to a particular ethnic group? On what basis is your ethnicity distinct from the larger culture? Do you feel that you are treated differently due to your ethnicity? Has your treatment been favorable or unfavorable? Explain.

2. Which of the three sociological models used to explain relations between dominant and minority groups appeals to you? Assimilation? Segregation? Cultural pluralism? Or, some combination of the three? Is it possible that instances of all three models are can be found in the U.S.? If so, please explain.

IV. KEY TERMS

Listed below are some of the key terms that are introduced in Chapter 10. After you have read the chapter in your text and worked through the overview on the preceding pages, test your recall by writing the definitions of the terms in the space provided. You may check your work by referring to the *Key Terms* section at the end of the chapter in your text.

acculturation_____
_____

cultural pluralism _____
_____

discrimination _____
_____

ethnicity _____
_____

minority group _____
_____

prejudice_____
_____

racism _____
_____

scapegoating_____
_____

segregation _____
_____

stereotyping _____
_____

V. TEST QUESTIONS

Multiple-Choice Questions
Choose the correct answer from the choices provided.

1.   Race refers to a category of people:
   a.   whose common social characteristics are believed to make them racially distinct.
   b.   whose common physical characteristics are believed to make them socially distinct.
   c.   who share the same ethnic heritage.
   d.   who belong to the same culture.

2. Which of the following is an aspect of ethnicity rather than race?
    a. hair texture
    b. skin color
    c. facial characteristics
    d. family background

3. The sociological significance of placing people in a particular racial or ethnic group derives from the fact that:
    a. once so labeled, a person is often treated differently.
    b. such categorizations make it possible to determine the racial and ethnic make-up of a particular culture.
    c. it then becomes possible for sociologists to explain social relations between various groups of people.
    d. none of the above.

4. Which of the following is true of "minority groups"?
    a. Minority groups are distinguished on the basis of perceived racial differences.
    b. Minority groups are distinguished on the basis of perceived cultural differences.
    c. Minority groups are disadvantaged as a result of their status within the larger culture.
    d. All of the above are true of minority groups.

5. The sociological model that best characterizes a group that retains its distinct cultural identity within a framework that assures its members' overall equality is:
    a. assimilation.
    b. segregation.
    c. cultural pluralism.
    d. acculturation.

6. Generalizing a set of characteristics to all members of a group is referred to as:
    a. scapegoating.
    b. racism.
    c. stereotyping.
    d. redlining.

7. According to government statisticians, "minorities" will account for what percent of the U.S. population by the year 2050?
    a. 10 percent
    b. 15 percent
    c. 25 percent
    d. 50 percent

8. Slavery was officially abolished in the U.S. in 1863 by the:
   a. Emancipation Proclamation.
   b. Jim Crow laws.
   c. Civil Rights legislation.
   d. bracero program.

9. Irish Americans, French Americans, and Italian Americans are:
   a. racial groups.
   b. ethnic groups.
   c. model minorities.
   d. new immigrants.

10. New immigrants to the U.S. are almost entirely:
    a. Asian.
    b. Latino and Asian.
    c. Latino and White Ethnic.
    d. Asian and African.

True/False Questions
For each of the following statements, decide whether the statement is true or false. Write your answer in the space provided.

_____ 1. Researchers have concluded that variations between racial categories are greater than variations within any racial categories.

_____ 2. Concepts of race are socially constructed within a given culture.

_____ 3. Affirmative action laws are no longer in effect in the U.S.

_____ 4. Blaming others for one's problems is a form of scapegoating.

_____ 5. Stereotypes can be positive or negative.

_____ 6. Racial and ethnic segregation are widespread in the U.S. despite Civil Rights legislation.

_____ 7. To be sociologically defined as a minority, a group must only differ on some characteristic from the rest of the population.

_____ 8. Job discrimination and redlining are forms of institutional discrimination.

_____ 9. From the cultural pluralist perspective, segregation can help to preserve ethnic communities.

_____ 10. Globalization has brought with it a decrease in acts of racial and ethnic violence.

Matching Exercise
For each of the following terms, identify the correct definition and write the appropriate letter in the space provided.

a.   assimilation
b.   ethnic economic enclaves
c.   ethnicity
d.   institutional discrimination
e.   minority group
f.   model minority
g.   race
h.   redlining
i.   scapegoating
j.   stereotyping

_____   1.   a category of people whose biologically-based common physical characteristics are believed to make them socially distinct.

_____   2.   neighborhoods comprised primarily of members of an immigrant ethnic group.

_____   3.   generalizing a set of characteristics to all members of a group.

_____   4.   in banking practice, figuratively drawing a line through an area to indicate that it is off-limits to lending activity.

_____   5.   blaming another person or group for one's problems.

_____   6.   unequal treatment that has become part of the routine operation of major social institutions.

_____   7.   absorption into the dominant mainstream culture.

_____   8.   the attribution of characteristics to groups of people who share a common cultural heritage.

_____   9.   a term used to refer to a group of people who are positively stereotyped as, for example, intelligent and hard-working--characteristics that are highly valued in American culture.

_____   10.   a group of people distinguished and disadvantaged on the basis of perceived racial or cultural differences from the dominant group in society.

Completion

Write in the word(s) that best completes each of the following statements. To check your work, you may refer to the answer key at the end of this study guide.

1.   Sociologists define _____ as a category of people whose biologically-based common physical characteristics are believed to make them socially distinct.

2.   The attribution of characteristics to groups of people who share a common cultural heritage is referred to as _____ .

3.   A _____ _____ consists of a group of people, distinguished on the basis of perceived racial or cultural differences from the dominant group, and who are disadvantaged as a result of their status.

4.   Of the three sociological models used to explain the relations between dominant and minority groups, _____ emphasizes the incorporation of minority groups into the mainstream American culture.

5.   _____ is the process by which immigrant groups come to adopt the norms, values, and life-ways of the dominant culture.

6.   According to the _____ _____ model, voluntary segregation of people into their own ethnic communities can help to preserve those communities.

7.   _____ is a preconceived belief about an individual or group, whereas _____ is unequal treatment of an individual or group based on their membership in some group.

8.   The "Jim Crow" laws mandated _____ in schools, restaurants, and public buildings, effectively defeating the political and economic progress made by African Americans during the nineteenth century.

9.   _____ _____ has resulted in unequal treatment of minorities in, for example, terms of jobs, housing, and education.

10.   The increased contact between different cultures and changing economic conditions brought about by globalization threatens the livelihoods of many people, increasing the possibilities for _____ -- blaming another person or group for one's problems.

CHAPTER 11

SEX AND GENDER

I. LEARNING OBJECTIVES

1. To define and become familiar with the concepts of sex, gender, and sexuality.
2. To become familiar with classical sociological and contemporary feminist theories of gender.
3. To learn about the ways in which gender roles are learned and reinforced through the various social institutions.
4. To become familiar with gender and social stratification.
5. To become familiar with issues surrounding violence against women.
6. To define heterosexuality and homosexuality.
7. To understand the impact of globalization on gender inequality.

II. CHAPTER OVERVIEW

In this chapter, you are introduced to the concepts and theories that organize sociological thinking about sex, gender, and human sexuality.

A. Most sociologists give greater weight to social influences than to biological influences in accounting for the behavioral differences between men and women.

   1. Sociologists use the term *sex* to refer to biological differences between men and women. Define *sex*, and give one or two examples to illustrate its biological emphasis.

   2. Sociologists use the term *gender* to refer to the social differences between men and women. Define *gender*, and briefly explain how it is socially constructed.

   3. Define *gender roles*. According to most sociologists, how are gender roles acquired?

   4. State the distinction made in your text regarding the terms "male" and "female" and "masculine" and "feminine."

5. Some research has sought to determine whether biological sex determines gender. What has this research concluded?

6. Define *gender identity*. When and how is one's gender identity acquired?

7. Briefly describe two studies that are mentioned in your text that provide evidence in support of the importance of socialization over biology in the acquisition of gender.

8. Define *sexuality*. What does it mean to say that sexuality, like gender, is socially constructed?

9. While there may be only two biological sexes, there is a range of behaviors associated with human sexuality. Define *sexual orientation*. List and define the four forms of human sexual orientation mentioned in your text.

	Orientation	Definition
a.		
b.		
c.		
d.		

B. **Sociological Theories About Gender.** In this section, you are introduced to two traditional sociological and feminists theories of gender.

1. Briefly explain how classical sociological theory views gender differences.

   a. How did the early classical theorists--Comte, Durkheim, Rousseau--view the role of women in society? How did they view the role of men in society?

b. Briefly explain how Talcott Parsons viewed the role differences between men and women.

c. According to Parsons, how are role differences acquired?

2. Define *feminism*, and explain its emergence in the U.S.

a. Define *sexism*. How does sexism contribute to the maintenance of patriarchy?

3. Three broad streams of feminist theory are presented in your text. List them below, and state their primary assumption concerning women's inequality.

<u>Feminist Theory</u>   <u>Assumption</u>

a.

b.

c.

4. Feminist thinking has contributed to our sociological understanding of *patriarchy*. Define *patriarchy*. What has anthropological research concluded about patriarchal societies?

5. Define *multicultural feminism*. How is multicultural feminism different from the three approaches mentioned above?

C. **Doing Gender: Learning Gender Roles.** In Chapter 10, the term *stereotype* means to generalize a set of characteristics to all members of a group. In this section, you will become familiar with the common stereotypes concerning men's and women's behavior, and how gender-appropriate roles are acquired.

1. Table 11.1 in your text lists some of the common stereotypes typically associated with masculine and feminine behaviors. List four stereotypes below.

    Masculine behaviors   Feminine behaviors
    _____   _____
    _____   _____
    _____   _____
    _____   _____

2. What does it mean to say that gender identity is "actively accomplished"?

3. Define the term *gender factory*, and explain why the family is considered a gender factory.

    a. What are some of the things that parents do or don't do that reinforce gender-stereotyped roles for their sons and daughters?

4. Briefly explain how peers can influence one's gender identity.

5. What are some of the ways in which gender stereotypes are reinforced through the media (television, magazines)?

6. In Chapter 5, you learned that schools are the source of a *hidden curriculum*--the unspoken socialization to norms, values, and roles that occurs in the classroom. What are some of the ways in which gender roles are reinforced in schools?

7. What evidence is there to suggest that the conventional gender stereotypes are breaking down in the media and in the schools?

D.   **Gender and Social Stratification.** In this section, you will become familiar with gender stratification in the U.S.--particularly that which occurs in the workplace, the home, and in the political sphere.

1.   How do social scientists explain the existence of gender stratification and inequality in society?

    a.   How did women's position and role in society change with the shift to modern industrial society?

2.   Briefly explain how the home is a domain in which gender stratification exists.

    a.   What is the *second shift*, and how does it contribute to gender stratification?

    b.   As compared to men, which group of women spends on average the greatest amount of time working at home and at paid employment per week? The least?

    c.   What evidence is there to suggest that inequality in the home is declining?

3.   The Industrial Revolution brought about a separation between home and workplace. What effect did this separation have on women's work role?

    a.   What is meant by the *feminization of labor*?

    b.   What reasons are given to explain the feminization of labor in the U.S.?

    c.   On average, what percentage of men's earnings do women workers earn?

d. What functionalist explanation is offered for why women earn less than men for the same job? What is the primary critique of this explanation?

e. What is an alternative explanation for why women earn less than men for the same job?

f. What is *triple oppression*? Who experiences triple oppression?

g. What is the *glass ceiling*? Describe the conditions that characterize occupations where women encounter a glass ceiling.

h. Define Rosabeth Moss Kanter's notion of *tokenism*? What are the effects of tokenism on women's work experience?

4. Describe the character of women's political participation in the U.S.

a. What explanations are offered to account for women's political participation?

b. What evidence is there to suggest that women are playing a more significant role in U.S. politics?

E. **Violence Against Women**

1. Define the term *rape*.

2.   List and define the forms of sexual relationship in Paulene Bart's classification system.

      <u>Form of sexual relationship</u>   <u>Definition</u>

      a.

      b.

      c.

      d.

3.   Why is it difficult to know home many rapes actually occur? What estimate does research give concerning the number of rapes that occur?

4.   Who commits rape?

5.   Define the term *rape culture*. How does male socialization contribute to a rape culture?

6.   Explain how rape is used as a political tool. Give an example from your text or one of your own to illustrate the political use of rape.

7.   How does the Federal Equal Employment Opportunity Commission define *sexual harassment*?

      a.   Under what workplace circumstances does sexual harassment typically occur?

      b.   What has research revealed about sexual harassment in schools?

c.   What did the 1991 Civil Rights Act do for victims of racial, religious, and sexual discrimination?

F.   **Homosexuality**

1.   Although most sociologists believe that homosexuality results from a combination of biological and social factors, some argue that biology plays a more critical role.

    a.   What evidence is offered to support the view that biological influences are more important?

    b.   What have twin studies concluded?

2.   Why is it difficult to accurately estimate the number of homosexuals in the U.S.?

3.   Define *homophobia*. According to a national public opinion survey, how do most Americans regard homosexuality and equal rights for homosexuals?

4.   Briefly describe the social movements that have fought for homosexual rights.

G.   **Globalization and Gender Inequality.** In this section, you will become familiar with the effects of globalization on gender relations and equality.

1.   How has globalization contributed to the feminization of labor around the world?

2.   Declining wages and the loss of well-paying jobs has meant an increase in the number of women entering the workforce around the world.

    a.   Describe the characteristics of the group of women who make up the female global workforce?

b.   Describe the working conditions under which these women work.

3.   Briefly explain how globalization has opened channels of communication between women around the world.

a.   The flow of information between women around the world has brought mixed results for women. How has the increased communication improved conditions for women?

b.   How has the increased communication worsened conditions for women in the former Soviet Union and Eastern Europe?

4.   How has globalization contributed to greater equality for homosexuals around the world?

III.   **STUDENT ACTIVITIES**

1.   Peers can have a strong impact on one's gender identity. As your text points out, failure to conform to peer expectations regarding gender can be stigmatizing, painful, and cruel. Think about your own gender socialization. Did you experience peer pressure to conform to stereotyped gender expectations as a child? How were gender roles reinforced and nonconforming behavior sanctioned? Have you experienced peer pressure to conform to gender roles as a adult? Does peer pressure to conform to stereotyped gender roles differ over time or across cultures?

2.   Some sociologists have argued that rape occurs because men are socialized to regard women as sex objects. Others, however, point out that men are also socialized into the norms and values that regard rape as deviant. Given these contradictory views, how would you explain the occurrence of rape or other forms of violence against women in your community? Do you believe that men are socialized to regard women as sex objects? If so, describe some of the ways in

which this sort of socialization occurs. What steps can be taken to reduce or prevent violence against women in your community?

IV.   KEY TERMS

Listed below are some of the key terms that are introduced in Chapter 11. After you have read the chapter in your text and worked through the overview on the preceding pages, test your recall by writing the definitions of the terms in the space provided. You may check your work by referring to the *Key Terms* section at the end of the chapter in your text.

feminization of labor _____

_____

gender_____

_____

gender role _____

_____

multicultural feminism _____

_____

patriarchy _____

_____

rape culture _____

_____

sex _____

_____

sexism_____

_____

tokenism_____

_____

triple oppression_____

_____

V. TEST QUESTIONS

Multiple-Choice Questions
Choose the correct answer from the choices provided.

1. According to the U.S. Census data, the average full-time woman worker earns approximately what percent of every dollar earned by a full-time male worker?
    a.   45 percent
    b.   53 percent
    c.   69 percent
    d.   80 percent

2. The normative expectations concerning gender appropriate behavior in a particular culture are called:
    a.   sex roles.
    b.   gender roles.
    c.   male and female roles.
    d.   socialized roles.

3. Which of the following statements is <u>false</u>?
    a.   Heterosexuality is the normative sexual orientation in all cultures.
    b.   Heterosexuality and homosexuality are the result of biological and social factors.
    c.   Specific behaviors associated with heterosexuality and homosexuality are socially learned.
    d.   Heterosexuality is biologically based, whereas homosexuality is socially based.

4. The viewpoint that women's inequality is the result of imperfect institutions that can be corrected by reform is held by:
    a.   liberal feminists.
    b.   multicultural feminists.
    c.   socialist feminists.
    d.   radical feminists.

5. Research has shown that:
    a.   all known societies have been patriarchal to some degree.
    b.   patriarchal social relations emerged as a consequence of the production of surplus.
    c.   patriarchal social relations emerged as a consequence of industrialization.
    d.   patriarchal social relations are not evident in modern society.

6. Sexism is based on the belief that women are:
    a.   innately superior to men.
    b.   innately inferior to men.
    c.   equal to men.
    d.   subordinate to men by choice.

7.	Research on learning gender roles has found that gender identity is:
	a.	biologically determined.
	b.	socially acquired.
	c.	fully acquired by the age of 5 or 6.
	d.	passively learned from others.

8.	The feminization of labor in the U.S. is a result of:
	a.	an increase in the number of women entering the labor force since the early 1970s.
	b.	a rise in the number of female-headed households.
	c.	an increase in the number of years women are living and a decrease in childbearing.
	d.	all of the above.

9.	Triple oppression refers to:
	a.	lower income women of color who experience discrimination and inequality based on their gender, race, and class status.
	b.	the problem of unequal pay for three groups of women in the U.S.--Black, Latino, and Asian.
	c.	three forms of discrimination found in the workplace--unequal pay for women, sexual harassment, and tokenism.
	d.	the three spheres of inequality for women--the workplace, the home, and politics.

10.	Research has shown that:
	a.	violence against women, including rape, is partly the result of male socialization.
	b.	most rapes are committed by relatives, acquaintances, or partners.
	c.	men are likely to regard rape as justified if the woman led him on by, for example, asking him out or letting him pay for the date.
	d.	all of the above.

True/False Questions
For each of the following statements, decide whether the statement is true or false. Write your answer in the space provided.

_____	1.	Sociologists give greater weight to social influences in accounting for the behavioral differences between men and women than to biological factors.

_____	2.	Most research has concluded that social learning, rather than biology, largely accounts for gender identity.

_____	3.	Human sexuality, unlike gender, is biologically determined.

_____	4.	Classical sociological theory argues that gender differences are normal and functional for society as a whole.

_____	5.	All feminists believe that patriarchy and sexism should be abolished.

_____ 6. The feminization of labor refers to the growing number of occupations that are stereotypically "feminine" in nature.

_____ 7. Most sociologists believe that discrimination, rather than conscious choice of occupation, is a major reason that women are paid less than men for the same jobs.

_____ 8. Sexual harassment typically occurs in situations of equal power between men and women.

_____ 9. Most sociologists believe that homosexuality results from a combination of biological factors and social learning.

_____ 10. Globalization has brought about a decrease in economic inequality for women around the world.

Matching Exercise

For each of the following terms, identify the correct definition and write the appropriate letter in the space provided.

a. bisexuality
b. gender identity
c. glass ceiling
d. radical feminism
e. rape
f. second shift
g. sexuality
h. sexual harassment
i. socialist feminism
j. transexuality

_____ 1. a seemingly invisible barrier to movement into the top positions in business and government, which makes it difficult for some women to reach the top of their professions.

_____ 2. any behavior that entails, for example, unwelcome conduct of a sexual nature when such conduct is used, for example, as a condition of employment; or when such conduct interferes with an individual's performance or contributes to an intimidating environment.

_____ 3. a stream of feminist thought that holds that women's inequality is fundamental to all other systems of inequality.

_____ 4. when the sexual identity of a person of one sex is with persons of the opposite sex.

_____ 5. the unpaid housework that women typically do after they come home from their paid employment.

_____ 6. sexual desire for persons of either sex.

_____ 7. the forcing of non-consensual vaginal, oral, or anal intercourse.

_____ 8. a stream of feminist thought that holds that women's inequality is largely the result of capitalist economic relations that must be transformed before women can achieve equality.

_____ 9. the ways in which individuals in a particular culture come to think of themselves as male or female.

_____ 10. the ways in which people construct their erotic or sexual relationships.

Completion
Write in the word(s) that best completes each of the following statements. To check your work, you may refer to the answer key at the end of this study guide.

1. _____ refers to anatomical or other biological differences between males and females, whereas _____ refers to behavioral differences that are culturally based and socially learned.

2. In _____ societies, women are treated as inferior to men, resulting in their subordinate economic position and political power.

3. While the _____ _____ _____ has resulted in a substantial increase in the number of women in the paid workforce, women typically occupy low-paying occupations and are paid less than men who hold similar occupations.

4. The prevalence of rape in American culture is partly the result of male socialization and has led some to conclude that the constant threat of rape contributes to a _____ _____.

5. _____ feminism focuses on understanding an ending inequality for all women, regardless of race, class, nationality, age, sexual orientation, or other characteristics.

6. Rosabeth Moss Kanter refers to the experience of women who have made it in a man's professional world as _____ -- where women are held up as representing all women, rather than being treated as individuals.

7.   _____ _____ typically occurs in situations of unequal power and can range from crude and explicit efforts to coerce an unwanted sexual relationship to subtle innuendoes that carry the same meaning.

8.   In the controversy surrounding the relative importance of nature and nurture in accounting for behavioral differences between men and women, sociologists give greater weight to _____ influences than to _____ factors.

9.   Cultures differ in their norms and values regarding _____ _____ -- the normative expectations concerning appropriately "masculine" or "feminine" behavior in a particular culture.

10.   _____ sociological theory holds that gender differences are both normal and functional for society as a whole.

CHAPTER 12

AGING

I.   LEARNING OBJECTIVES

1.   To understand how American society is "graying" and its likely impact on future generations.
2.   To become familiar with the sociological perspectives on aging and the various explanations of aging.
3.   To understand aging and inequality in the United States.
4.   To understand how the world population is "graying" and to explore the impact of globalization on the elderly.

II.   CHAPTER OVERVIEW

In this chapter, you will explore the nature of aging in American society, including the concepts and theories that organize sociological thinking about the aging of American society and the world population.

A.   **The Graying of American Society.** American society and other industrial societies are steadily growing older--a phenomenon that is referred to as "graying."

    1.   What does it mean for a society to be "graying"?

    2.   What factors contribute to the graying of America and the world population?

    3.   What is the average life expectancy for American males and females? By way of contrast, what is the average life expectancy for men and women of most African countries?

    4.   There are significant racial and ethnic differences in the "graying" of America.

        a.   According to Table 12.2, which group of Americans has the largest percent of their population over the age of 65? Which group of Americans has the smallest percent of their population over the age of 65? How is the difference in the size of the two elderly populations explained?

B.   **Sociological Perspectives on Aging.** While the process of aging is clearly linked to the biological changes that take place over one's lifespan, aging is very much shaped by social factors. In this section, you are introduced to the biological, psychological, and social perspectives on aging.

1.   Before exploring the various perspectives on aging, it will be useful to define some of the key concepts used in this area of sociology.

   a.   How is *aging* sociologically defined? What are the three processes that affect us as we age?

   b.   Define *chronological age*. How is chronological age important in understanding aging?

   c.   What is *social gerontology*? What difficulty arises in studies of social gerontology?

2.   *Biological aging* refers to the physical effects of aging that occur throughout the lifespan.

   a.   What are some of the biological effects of aging?

   b.   What are some of the common stereotypes about the biological changes that take place as we age?

3.   *Psychological aging* primarily refers to the mental or psychological effects that are associated with aging.

   a.   Much more is known about the physical effects of aging than the psychological effects. What are some of the psychological effects that are commonly associated with aging?

b.   What are some of the common misconceptions about the psychological effects of aging?

4.   *Social aging* refers to the cultural norms, values, and roles that are associated with a particular chronological age.

     a.   Define the term *life course*.

     b.   Although patterns of social aging vary widely by gender, race, ethnicity, and over time, what are the roles associated with a "typical" American life course?

5.   Define *retirement*. What is the official age of retirement in the U.S.? Briefly describe the effects of retirement on older adults.

C.   **Sociological Explanations of Aging.** In this section, you will become familiar with the sociological theories of aging.

1.   Briefly describe the first generation functionalist approach to aging.

     a.   Briefly describe *disengagement theory*. According to this theory, how is the "disengagement" of the elderly functional for society?

     b.   What challenge does *activity theory* present to disengagement theory?

     c.   What is the primary critique of functionalist theories of aging?

2.   What is the main emphasis of the second generation stratification and conflict theories of aging?

a.   How do social conflict theorists view the impact of gender, race, class, and globalization on the elderly?

b.   What is the primary critique of social conflict theories of aging?

3.   What is the primary emphasis of the third generation multi-faceted approach to aging?

a.   What critique does the multi-faceted approach make of other approaches to aging? What alternative does the multi-faceted approach offer?

D.   **Government Support for the Elderly: Medicare and Social Security.** The rapid increase in the elderly population has placed ever-greater demands on governmental programs that provide social and economic support to Americans. In this section, you will become familiar with two programs that provide support for the elderly.

1.   How are *Medicare* and *Social Security* financed? Who is eligible for Medicare and/or Social Security funding?

a.   What services does Medicare funding support? Social Security?

b.   How do women's monthly benefits under Social Security compare to men's?

E.   **Aging and Inequality in the United States.** Although Social Security and Medicare help to reduce economic inequality among the elderly, many elderly still face problems of poverty, social isolation, ageism, physical abuse, and health.

1.   What percentage of the elderly population live in poverty? How does this figure compare to American society as a whole? How does it compare to children under the age of 16?

a.   Poverty rates vary considerably by race. Which group has the lowest percent of their elderly population in poverty? Which group has the greatest percent of their elderly population in poverty?

2.   A common stereotype about the elderly is that they remain isolated from human contact. Describe the experience of men and women over the age of 60 as it relates to their relative lifespan and living arrangements.

a.   What is the norm in American society concerning the family's obligation to provide support for the elderly and adult children?

b.   What factors may contribute to increased isolation among the elderly?

3.   Define *ageism*.

a.   What are some common stereotypes concerning the elderly?

b.   What reasons are given to explain the existence of prejudice against the elderly?

4.   Although it is difficult to estimate the number of elderly who are abused, how common is elderly abuse thought to be?

a.   A common stereotype is that elder abuse results from the anger and resentment adult children feel toward their dependent parents. What does research suggest to be the actual reasons for elderly abuse?

5.   Although most elderly people rate their health as reasonably good, what are some of the health problems that come with advancing age?

       a.   What concerns have researchers voiced regarding the growing elderly population and the provision of health coverage?

6.   What special difficulties do gay and lesbian elderly face?

       a.   What evidence is there to suggest that the situation is improving for elderly homosexuals?

F.   **The Politics of Aging**

1.   Define the term *generational equity*.

       a.   With a growing elderly population, what concerns arise with regard to generational equity?

       b.   What is the purpose and main argument of the organization Americans for Generational Equity (AGE)?

G.   **Lifelong Learning**. In this section, you will become familiar with learning as a lifelong process--one that carries forward into advanced old age.

1.   Define the terms *andragogy* and *geragogy*.

       a.   How do these methods of learning differ from conventional methods?

H. **Globalization: The "Graying" of the World Population.** Many of factors that have contributed to the "graying" of American society have contributed to the "graying" of the world population.

   1. What is the world's average life expectancy anticipated to be by the year 2025? How many people are anticipated to be over the age of 65 by 2025?

      a. What is the primary concern that arises with the "graying" of the world population?

      b. In what ways has globalization begun to change treatment of the elderly throughout the world?

III. STUDENT ACTIVITIES

   1. List some of the concerns that arise with the ever-increasing elderly world population. What can be done to meet these concerns? What economic or social services should be provided to support the elderly? Who should be responsible for supporting the elderly--the family, the government, the working population, or the elderly themselves?

   2. Which of the sociological theories of aging is most appealing to you? Do you agree or disagree with the functionalist view that the elderly should disengage from an active role in society? Or, do you agree with funtionalist activity theory that the elderly contribute to society by remaining active? What argument can you make in support of the social conflict theory of aging? Do you believe that the problems of aging are related to other sources of inequality in society?

IV. KEY TERMS

Listed below are some of the key terms that are introduced in Chapter 12. After you have read the chapter in your text and worked through the overview on the preceding pages, test your recall by writing the definitions of the terms in the space provided. You may check your work by referring to the *Key Terms* section at the end of the chapter in your text.

activity theory_____

_____

ageism _____

_____

aging _____

_____

andragogy_____

_____

chronological age _____

_____

disengagement theory_____

_____

generational equity _____

_____

graying (of America) _____

_____

social age _____

_____

V.   TEST QUESTIONS

Multiple-Choice Questions
Choose the correct answer from the choices provided.

1.   According to U.S. Bureau of Census data, which group has the largest proportion of persons over the age of 65?
    a.   Whites
    b.   Hispanics
    c.   Blacks
    d.   Native Americans

2.   The sociological definition of aging is based on:
    a.   biological factors.
    b.   psychological factors.
    c.   social factors.
    d.   biological, psychological, and social factors.

3.   The "graying" of America is a result of:
    a.   increased life expectancy.
    b.   decreased infant mortality.
    c.   both a and b
    d.   increased opportunity for individuals to remain employed well into old age.

4. Social gerontology is complicated by the fact that:
   a. culturally-defined values, norms, and roles regarding age change over time.
   b. the elderly are a highly homogeneous group.
   c. the elderly are socially isolated.
   d. most elderly persons experience the loss of the mental capability to participate in social research.

5. The idea that the elderly should pull back from social roles, freeing up those roles for others, is from:
   a. activity theory.
   b. disengagement theory.
   c. social gerontology.
   d. conflict theory.

6. The two principal sources of support for the elderly--Social Security and Medicare--are financed through:
   a. workers' payroll deductions.
   b. employer contributions.
   c. taxes on self-employed workers.
   d. all of the above

7. Which of the following statements is <u>false</u> concerning aging and poverty in the U.S.?
   a. The rate of poverty among people over 65 is higher than for American society as a whole.
   b. The rate of poverty among people over 65 is lower than for American society as a whole.
   c. The rate of poverty among people over 65 is higher than for middle-aged working people.
   d. The rate of poverty among people over 65 is lower than for children under 16 years of age.

8. Ageism refers to:
   a. the study of aging.
   b. prejudice based on age.
   c. the psychological processes that occur as one ages.
   d. the "graying" of the world population.

9. Research suggests that physical abuse of the elderly:
   a. is less widespread than commonly perceived.
   b. is more widespread than commonly perceived.
   c. results from the anger and resentment adult children feel toward their dependent parents.
   d. occurs because the elderly are typically frail, dependent, and vulnerable.

10. Striking a balance between the needs and interests of members of different generations is referred to as:
    a. geragogy
    b. andragogy
    c. generational equity
    d. social gerontology

True/False Questions

For each of the following statements, decide whether the statement is true or false. Write your answer in the space provided.

_____ 1. There are no significant racial or ethnic differences in the "graying" of the American population.

_____ 2. Research has shown that most people do not follow a "typical" life course from infancy to old age.

_____ 3. The idea of a fixed age at which one retires from paid employment began during pre-industrial society.

_____ 4. According to the social conflict view, the problems of aging related to sources of inequality that are systematically produced through the routine operation of social institutions.

_____ 5. The rate of poverty among people over 65 is lower than for American society as a whole.

_____ 6. Ageism refers to prejudice based on age.

_____ 7. Activity theory of aging holds that active people--including the elderly--are more likely to lead fulfilling and productive lives.

_____ 8. Promoters of generational equity argue that people who are currently working are being unfairly taxed to support a growing retired population.

_____ 9. Older adult learning, geragogy, provides information in the standard undergraduate classroom format.

_____ 10. Most societies in the world today are experiencing an aging of their populations as a result of declining birth and death rates.

Matching Exercise

For each of the following terms, identify the correct definition and write the appropriate letter in the space provided.

a.   activity theory
b.   ageism
c.   aging
d.   chronological age
e.   disengagement theory
f.   generational equity
g.   geragogy
h.   life course
i.   social age
j.   social gerontology

_____   1.   a functionalist theory of aging that holds that elderly people should progressively pull back from social roles, freeing up those roles for others.

_____   2.   a discipline concerned with the study of the social aspects of aging.

_____   3.   the norms, values, and roles that are culturally associated with a particular chronological age.

_____   4.   the combination of biological, psychological, and social processes that affect people as they grow older.

_____   5.   a functionalist theory of aging that holds that active people are more likely to lead fulfilling and productive lives.

_____   6.   prejudice based on age.

_____   7.   the length of time a person has been alive.

_____   8.   a sequence of roles one is expected to assume as one ages.

_____   9.   the effort to strike a balance between the needs and interests of members of different generations.

_____   10.   older adult learning.

Completion

Write in the word(s) that best completes each of the following statements. To check your work, you may refer to the answer key at the end of this study guide.

1. The United States and other industrial societies are said to be _____ as an increasing proportion of their populations become elderly.

2. _____ is the combination of biological, psychological, and social processes that affect us as we grow older, whereas _____ _____ refers to the length of time a person has been alive.

3. _____ is a learning process that emphasizes building on the extensive life experience of older people.

4. Lowered physical viability, greater vulnerability to illness, and the loss of skin elasticity are examples of the _____ effects of aging.

5. _____ _____ is constructed within a particular culture and refers to the norms, values, and roles that are associated with a particular chronological age.

6. The sequence of roles one is expected to assume as one chronologically ages is referred to as the _____ _____.

7. Promoters of _____ _____ argue that a decreasing working population is being unfairly taxed to pay for a growing retired population.

8. According to _____ theory, the increasing frailty, illness, and dependency of elderly people leads them to progressively pull back from social roles.

9. The belief that the elderly are infirm, forgetful, dependent, senile, and other negative stereotypes are examples _____.

10. According to _____ theory, problems of aging are related to other sources of inequality in society, including those based on class, gender, and ethnicity.

PART IV

SOCIAL INSTITUTIONS

CHAPTER 13

POLITICS AND STATE

I.   LEARNING OBJECTIVES

1.   To become familiar with the major characteristics of the modern nation-state and to distinguish it from earlier forms of political organization.
2.   To become familiar with the types of state power and authority.
3.   To become familiar with the functionalist and social conflict theories of state power.
4.   To understand the various forms of governance: authoritarianism, totalitarianism, and democracy.
5.   To become acquainted with the American political system.
6.   To become familiar with war and the role of the military in American society.
7.   To understand the impact of globalization on governance in the modern world.

II.   CHAPTER OVERVIEW

In this chapter, you are introduced to the emergence and characteristics of the modern nation state, including the various forms of state power and authority. Particular attention is given to the various forms of governance found in modern society.

A.   **The Modern Nation-State and the Rule of Law**.   In this section, you will define the term *nation-state* and will learn about the unique features that distinguish modern nation-states from earlier forms of political organization.

   1.   How do sociologists define the terms *state* and *nation*? Explain how the term "legitimate" is understood in the definition of the state.

      a.   What is a *nation-state?*

      b.   There are several distinguishing features of the modern nation-state. Briefly explain or give the definition of the italicized characteristics of the modern nation-state, and then describe how they were expressed in earlier forms of political organization.

         <u>Modern Nation-State</u>   <u>Earlier Political Organizations</u>

         Complete authority

Law

Citizens

c. List and define the forms of citizenship rights mentioned in your text.

(1)

(2)

(3)

d. Define the term *nationalism*. Briefly explain how can nationalism threaten or strengthen a nation state.

B. **Power in the Modern Nation-State.** In this section, you will explore the relationship between power and authority in different societies, and become familiar with sociological theories of state power.

1. In Chapter 6, *power* was defined as the ability to mobilize resources and achieve a goal despite the resistance of others. Define *legitimate authority*, a particular type of power identified by Max Weber.

a. List and define the three types of legitimate authority identified by Weber. Briefly explain how rulers within each category claim the right to rule, and give an example illustrating each type of authority system.

Authority Type	Definition	Right to Rule	Example
(1)			
(2)			
(3)			

b. According to Weber, what problem can arise for the modern nation-state under charismatic authority? Provide an example illustrating this point.

2.   Briefly explain the main thesis of functionalist theories of the state.

        a.   According to functionalist theory, what is the role of the state?

        b.   While functionalist theories of state power assumed a high degree of
                consensus on society's norms and values, contemporary functionalist
                theory argues that modern societies are *pluralistic*. What is a *pluralistic*
                society? What is the role of government in pluralistic societies?

        c.   Briefly explain Robert Dahl's contribution to the functionalist view of
                political decision-making and governmental influence, including an
                explanation of *interest groups* and how a plurality of interest groups
                creates the possibility for *countervailing powers.*

        d.   What are the primary critiques of functionalist theory of state power?

3.   Briefly explain the main thesis of social conflict theories of the state.

        a.   Social conflict theory owes much to the writings of Karl Marx. According
                to Marx, what is the role of government in society?

        b.   The different streams of social conflict theory each emphasize a different
                relationship between the government and society's class structure. What is
                the main argument of *class dominance theory*?

        c.   Briefly describe G. William Domhoff's contribution to sociological
                understanding of political power in America.

d.   According to Domhoff, who are the power elite?

e.   Briefly explain how *structural contradiction* theory views the relationship between government and society's class structure.

f.   The writings of Max Weber and Karl Marx form the basis of the social conflict theory that emphasizes the *relative autonomy of the state*. What is the main argument of this version of social conflict theory?

4.   What is the primary critique of social conflict theories of the state?

C.   **Forms of Governance in the Modern World.** In this section, you will become familiar with the three forms of governance in modern society.

1.   Briefly describe the *authoritarian* political system.

a.   Describe the *monarchy* political system. Give an example of a society that exemplifies this form of governance.

b.   What is a *dictatorship*? How are most modern authoritarian dictatorship systems ruled?

2.   Describe the *totalitarian* political system. Give an example of a society that exemplifies this form of governance.

a.   How do totalitarian governments regulate and control people's public and private lives?

b. How do totalitarian governments derive their legitimacy?

3. Describe the *democratic* political system, and explain the origin of this system of government. What type of authority are democratic systems based on?

a. Define *direct democracy*, and explain the origin of the concept of democracy. Why is direct democracy not possible in modern society?

b. What is *representative democracy*?

4. How does a country's form of governance relate to its economic system?

a. On the following chart, briefly characterize the types of economic systems found in democratic, authoritarian, and totalitarian regimes.

Political regime	Economic system	
	Capitalist	Socialist
Democratic		
Authoritarian		
Totalitarian		

D. **The American Political System.** In this section, you are introduced to the American political system, including the party system, voting, and how the vote can be influenced by powerful groups.

1. Give the names of the two major political parties in the United States.

a.   Why is there little difference between the two major political parties in the United States?

2.   What is a *third party*, and what role does it play in national politics?

3.   Briefly explain the difference between the American electoral system and *parliamentary* system of government.

4.   How does the system of voting in the United States silence minority voices?

5.   What reasons are given for voter apathy in the United States? Which groups are most likely to be silent at election time?

6.   What role does the Supreme Court play in the American political system?

7.   Money, interest groups, and social movements play an important role in politics. Briefly explain the importance of money in determining the outcome of, for example, presidential or congressional elections.

a.   What is a *Political Action Committee (PAC)*? Explain the difference between a *pragmatic* PAC and an *ideological* PAC.

b.   Define and explain the role of *lobbyists* in American politics.

E.   **War and the Military.** In this section, you will become familiar with the role of the military in American society and the world.

1. The importance of the military and its role in American society is evident in the emergence of the *military industrial complex*. What is the military industrial complex?

   a. What agencies or organizations comprise the military industrial complex?

   b. How is military spending tied to particular local economies?

2. For a quarter century following World War II, the United States and the former Soviet Union pursued identical military strategies termed *Mutual Assured Destruction (MAD)*. What is Mutual Assured Destruction, and what purpose did it serve?

3. Although progress has been made to reduce the threat of nuclear warfare, *nuclear proliferation* remains a danger. What is nuclear proliferation? Which countries possess nuclear capabilities?

4. How many "official" wars has the United States been involved in over its two hundred year history? Among those wars, which claimed the greatest number of American lives?

   a. Why is modern conventional warfare almost as destructive as nuclear warfare?

5. Which two countries have been most heavily involved in arms sales?

   a. What is *peacetime conversion*, and why is it so difficult to achieve?

F. **Globalization: Toward a World Political Community?** In this section, you will explore how the growing interdependence among nations brought about by globalization has increased the possibility for a unified international system of rules and laws.

1. What is the main argument of the *institutionalist school of organizational theory*?

    a. According to the institutionalist school, why is institutional convergence thought to be compatible with democratic forms of governance?

    b. Explain how the emergence of regional trading blocks -- the European Community (EC) and the North American Free Trade Agreement (NAFTA) -- contribute to a global system of governance.

    c. Box 13.4 in your text discusses the possibility of a single world government. What are some of the signs that suggest that a single world government is possible? What are some of the obstacles to a single world government?

III. STUDENT ACTIVITIES

1. The end of the Cold War and the subsequent reduction in the nuclear arsenals held by the United States and the former Soviet Union has given some indication that the arms race is declining. Yet nuclear proliferation remains a danger as other countries develop their nuclear weapon capabilities. Do you think such strategies as Mutual Assured Destruction (MAD) are a viable solution to ensure that a nuclear war will not occur in the future? Do you think such strategies are worth the extreme risk and cost? What other strategies might be possible to reduce the threat of nuclear war?

2. One characteristic of the modern nation-state is that the members are thought of as citizens who are part of a political community in which they are granted certain rights and privileges. Such citizenship includes political rights, the assurance that one can participate in governance if one so chooses. The American poltical system, however, is presently characterized by widespread citizen indifference and apathy, reflected in low levels of voter turnout. Why do you think people choose

not to vote? What solutions would you suggest to increase voter participation in local or national elections?

IV.   KEY TERMS

Listed below are some of the key terms that are introduced in Chapter 13. After you have read the chapter in your text and worked through the overview on the preceding pages, test your recall by writing the definitions of the terms in the space provided. You may check your work by referring to the *Key Terms* section at the end of the chapter in your text.

authoritarianism _____

_____

charismatic authority _____

_____

dictatorship_____

_____

direct democracy _____

_____

legitimate authority _____

_____

nation-state_____

_____

nationalism _____

_____

power _____

_____

rational-legal authority _____

_____

traditional authority _____

_____

TEST QUESTIONS

Multiple-Choice Questions
Choose the correct answer from the choices provided.

1.   Which of the following is <u>not</u> a characteristic of the modern nation-state?
   a.   complete authority over its members
   b.   traditional beliefs that dictate how people should behave and how disputes are settled
   c.   a citizenry who are granted certain rights and privileges
   d.   a codified system of law

2.   Ideally, citizenship rights in the modern nation-state include:
   a.   civil rights.
   b.   social rights.
   c.   political rights.
   d.   all of the above

3.   Rational-legal authority is based on:
   a.   long-standing custom and habit.
   b.   the perceived inspirational qualities of the leader.
   c.   the perceived rationality of the leader.
   d.   the belief in the lawfulness of enacted rules.

4.   Functionalist theory of the state argues that:
   a.   the role of the state is to neutrally mediate between a plurality of contending interests, in which the influence of one group is offset by the interests of another.
   b.   the state serves the interests of the most powerful groups in society.
   c.   there is a unified upper class power elite that exerts control over politics, the economy, and the military.
   d.   aspects of social structure are mutually incompatible with one another and, therefore, result in structural instability.

5.   Social conflict theories of the state are derived primarily from the ideas of:
   a.   Max Weber.
   b.   Emile Durkheim.
   c.   Karl Marx.
   d.   C. Wright Mills.

6.   According to sociologist G. William Domhoff, power in American society is:
   a.   ruled by a ruling elite.
   b.   a pluralism of different groups with conflicting values and interests.
   c.   manifest when individuals with common concerns coalesce into interest groups to influence governmental policy.
   d.   characterized by a high degree of consensus on important beliefs and values.

7. Which of the following is <u>not</u> a form of governance in modern society?
    a. monarchy
    b. authoritarianism
    c. direct democracy
    d. democracy

8. The American political system is characterized by:
    a. the existence of only two major political parties.
    b. an electoral college voting system.
    c. representative democracy.
    d. all of the above.

9. A political system in which citizens elect representatives who are supposed to make decisions that express the wishes of the majority who elected them is called:
    a. direct democracy.
    b. representative democracy.
    c. parliamentary government.
    d. none of the above.

10. President Dwight D. Eisenhower coined this term to refer to the coalition of military and economic organizations who share an interest in weapons and other defense spending.
    a. Military Industrial Complex
    b. Mutual Assured Destruction
    c. United Nations
    d. North American Free Trade Agreement (NAFTA)

True/False Questions

For each of the following statements, decide whether the statement is true or false. Write your answer in the space provided.

_____   1. Many modern nation-states are comprised of people of different cultural, ethnic, or religious backgrounds.

_____   2. One characteristic of the modern nation-state is that it does not claim complete and final authority over its members.

_____   3. Politics in democratic societies is structured around competing political parties whose purpose is to gain control of the government by winning elections.

_____   4. Most democratic countries practice representative democracy rather than direct democracy.

_____ 5. The American political system is presently characterized by high levels of voter turnout.

_____ 6. Military spending has dropped in the United States.

_____ 7. The institutionalist school of organizational theory argues that globalization is reflected in the degree of divergence between the political institutions of the world's nations.

_____ 8. Countervailing powers theory holds that the influence of one group is offset by that of another.

_____ 9. Nazi Germany, the former Soviet Union during Stalin's regime, and Saddam Hussein's regime in Iraq are examples of totalitarian forms of governance.

_____ 10. Karl Marx is credited with identifying three "ideal types" of legitimate authority.

Matching Exercise
For each of the following terms, identify the correct definition and write the appropriate letter in the space provided.

a. citizens
b. civil rights
c. class dominance theory
d. countervailing powers
e. ethno-nationalism
f. interest groups
g. lobbyists
h. pluralism
i. rational-legal authority
j. state

_____ 1. a political theory, derived from the ideas of Karl Marx, that argues that there is a more-or-less unified upper class power elite that exerts control over politics, the economy, and the military.

_____ 2. a strongly-held set of beliefs based on identification with an ethnic community that calls for nationhood based on ethnic ties.

_____ 3. individuals who are part of a political community in which they are granted certain rights and privileges, while at the same time having specified obligations and duties.

_____ 4. a political theory that holds that society is comprised of groups with different and often conflicting values and interests on specific issues, that contend with one another on roughly equal footing.

_____ 5. a political apparatus possessing the legitimate monopoly over the use of force within its territory.

_____ 6. a theory that holds that the influence of one group is offset by that of another.

_____ 7. paid professionals whose job is to influence legislation.

_____ 8. power based on a belief in the lawfulness of enacted rules and the legitimate right of leaders to exercise authority through law.

_____ 9. groups comprised of people who share the same concerns on a particular issue and, therefore, unite in an effort to influence governmental policy.

_____ 10. legal rights that protect citizens from injuries perpetrated by other individuals and institutions.

Completion
Write in the word(s) that best completes each of the following statements. To check your work, refer to the answer key at the end of this study guide.

1. Between the 1950s and the 1980s, tension between the United States and the Soviet Union escalated sharply. This time came to be called the _____ _____.

2. With few exceptions, the _____ is the only form of statehood found throughout the modern world.

3. Underlying the organization of modern nation-states is a codified system of _____ that is established by the government and backed by the threat of force.

4. Citizenship rights in the modern nation-state can take several forms. _____ rights protect citizens from injuries perpetrated by other individuals and institutions, _____ rights call for governmental provision of various forms of economic and social security, and _____ rights assure that one can participate in governance if one so chooses.

5. _____ authority is based on a belief in the lawfulness of enacted rules and the legitimate right of leaders to exercise authority under such rules.

6. Contemporary functionalist theory argues that modern societies are _____, in that they are comprised of groups with different and often conflicting values and interests on specific issues, that contend with one another on roughly equal footing.

7.   _____ _____ theory was introduced by C. Wright Mills, who argued that there is a more-or-less unified power elite that exerts control over politics, the economy, and the military.

8.   A monarchy is an example of an _____ political system in which ordinary members of society are denied the right to participate in government.

9.   Under _____ democracy, all citizens fully participate in their own governance, whereas under _____ democracy, citizens elect representatives who are supposed to make decisions on their behalf.

10.   The _____ _____ of government is a type of democracy in which the chief of state is the head of the party with the largest number of representatives in the legislature.

CHAPTER 14

FAMILIES

I.   LEARNING OBJECTIVES

1.   To become familiar with the sociological definition of family.
2.   To understand the basic concepts used by social scientists in the study of the family.
3.   To become familiar with the functionalist and social conflict theories of the family.
4.   To understand how the family and family values have changed over the years.
5.   To appreciate the variety of family structures that are found in modern society.
6.   To explore the family differences based on race, class, and ethnicity.
7.   To understand the impact of globalization on the family.

II.   CHAPTER OVERVIEW

In this chapter, you are introduced to the theories and concepts that organize sociological thinking about the family. You will explore how families within different societies and cultures are structured, as well as how variations in race, class, and ethnicity shape the American family.

A.   **What is a family?**   This section begins by pointing out the difficulties that arise for sociologists as they attempt to define and study the family.

    1.   Why is it difficult to arrive at a definition of *family*?

    2.   How do sociologists and anthropologists define *family*?

B.   **Basic Concepts in the Study of the Family**. In this section, you will be introduced to the basic concepts that are used in the study of the family.

    1.   Just as with the concept of family, *marriage* is a culturally constructed concept. Give the sociological definition of *marriage*.

        a.   How is marriage is culturally constructed?

b. The most common family form in the United States is the *nuclear family*. Define *nuclear family*. What percentage of American households are thought to be nuclear family households?

c. What other family structures are possible?

d. What is an *extended family*, and among which groups are they more commonly found?

e. In western European societies, biological parents typically assume responsibility for child rearing. Define and discuss the reasoning behind the *child-minding* practices common among some families.

f. There are cultural differences in the number of wives or husbands a person may have. List and define the two basic cultural patterns, and state whether they are more common to industrial or preindustrial society.

Cultural pattern	Definition	Type of society
(1)		
(2)		

g. In most societies, marriages are *endogamous*. Define the term *endogamous*, and describe some of the ways in which endogamy is achieved.

C. **Theoretical Perspectives on Families.** In this section, you are introduced to the functionalist and social conflict theories of the family.

1. What is the underlying assumption of the functionalist theory of the family?

a. What are the three primary functions of the family?

(1)

(2)

(3)

b. What are some of the other functions the family provides for society as a whole?

c. What is the primary critique of the functionalist theory of the family?

2. What is the underlying assumption of the social conflict theory of the family?

a. Define and explain how the family is viewed as a *gender factory*.

b. What is the primary critique of the social conflict theory of the family?

D. **The Family in Modern Society.** In this section, you will become familiar with the ways in which the family's role in the larger society has changed over time.

1. The industrial revolution made a significant impact on the economic role of the family. Briefly explain the primary role of the family in preindustrial society, especially in agricultural based society.

a. What changes to family roles and social relations were brought about with industrialization?

b. How did the role of children change with industrialization?

2.   How has the family become a "haven of intimacy"?

      a.   Use the chart below to compare the arrangement of marriage and the primary bases for marriage in preindustrial and industrial societies.

	How Marriage Arranged	Basis for Marriage
(1) Preindustrial		
(2) Industrial		

E.   **Changing Family Values.** As your text makes clear, there is enormous diversity of opinion about "traditional family values" by race, class, ethnicity, religion, and gender. Moreover, family values change over time as society changes. In this section, you will become familiar with some of the ways in which sociologists think about and study family values in modern society.

1.   How have family values changed since the 1940-1950s?

      a.   Provide an example from your text or of your own illustrating how family values have changed over time.

2.   Define the term *marriage rate*, and explain how marriage rate in the United States has changed since the 1960s.

      a.   What are some of the sociological explanations for the changes that have taken place in marriage patterns in the United States?

      b.   How has women's economic independence affected their marital decisions?

c. Consider Figure 14.2 in your text. What percent of women are in the labor force. What reason is there to believe that women's labor force participation has peaked?

3. Define the term *divorce rate*, and list the countries that have the highest rates of divorce.

    a. What affect has the 'aging' of the U.S. population had on the divorce rate?

    b. List the three reasons given for the high divorce rate in the United States.

        (1)

        (2)

        (3)

4. Single parenting is not a new experience for American families. How do the reasons given for the occurrence of single parenting at the turn of the century differ from the reasons for the occurrence of single parenting today?

    a. Answer the following questions using Table 14.1, "Households of Children Under 18, by Race and Hispanic Origin, 1993."

        (1) Which group has the most children living with both parents? The fewest children living with both parents?

        (2) Which group has the most children living with mother only? The fewest number of children living with mother only?

5. Use the chart below to list some of the positive and negative effects of divorce and single parenting on women.

    Positive effects   Negative effects

    _____   _____

_____   _____

_____   _____

_____   _____

a.   What has research revealed concerning the economic effect of divorce on women?

6.   A number of studies have explored the impact of divorce and single parenting on children. What has most research concluded regarding the impact of divorce on children's well-being?

a.   What percent of all children living in female-headed households live in poverty?

b.   What effect does the economic stress associated wtih divorce and single parenting have on children's education and school performance?

c.   What arguments run counter to the finding that children of divorced families have greater behavioral problems?

7.   In 1950, five percent of all births were to unwed mothers. What percent of all births are to unwed mothers today?

a.   What percent of all births to unwed mothers are white? What percent of all births to unwed mothers are black? Among what age groups do most births to unwed mothers occur?

b.   What factors account for the increase in births to single women?

182

8.   Define *cohabitation*, and list some of the reasons cohabitation has increased.

9.   While most homosexual couples desire stable and long-lasting family relationships, this goal can be difficult to achieve. List some of the barriers homosexual couples encounter in establishing routine family relations.

10.   Remarriage often leads to the formation of "blended" step families. What is a "blended" step family?

      a.   What are some of the difficulties children face in the formation of step families?

      b.   What difficulties arise with respect to the norms that govern remarriage?

F.   **Racial and Ethnic diversity in the American Family.** In this section, you are introduced to many of the family differences associated with social class, race, and ethnicity.

      1.   Box 14.2 in your text, "Silenced Voices: Deaf Culture and 'Hearing' Families," illustrates the diversity of American families. Briefly explain the argument made by many in the deaf community that the meaning of deafness be redefined. What is the reasoning behind this argument?

      2.   One way in which families differ by social class is in their attitudes toward children's independence. Briefly explain the relative value placed on independence by middle and upper class American families as compared to working class families.

a. Sociologist Melvin Kohn has studied class differences in child-rearing for many years. What does Kohn attribute class differences in child-rearing to?

3. Table 14.2 indicates that the percentage of African Americans who have never married is almost twice the percentage of whites who have never married. How is the marriage rate among African Americans explained?

a. Tables 14.2 and 14.3 indicate significant differences between white and black families with regard to marital status and household make-up. List some of the factors that contribute to these differences.

b. What is the Moynihan Report? Briefly explain why the Moynihan Report is so controversial.

c. Consider Critical Thinking Box 14.3, "The Politics of Studying the Black Family." How does sociologist William Julius Wilson explain the family pattern differences between blacks and whites?

4. Although the Latino ethnic category is comprised of many different cultures, there are some distinct family characteristics that can be generalized across this group. List some of the cultural characteristics of Latino families mentioned in your text.

a. How are the cultural characteristics of Latino families reflected in the divorce and marriage rates and incidence of single parenting among this group?

5. List some of the cultural characteristics of Asian American families.

6. Although there are nearly 500 different American Indian nations, many American Indian families display similar characteristics. What are some of the characteristics of Native American families?

G. **Domestic Violence**

1. Define *domestic violence*.

    a. Why is it difficult to obtain accurate information on domestic violence?

    b. In the 1970s, Murray Straus proposed that violence within families was so extensive that it could be regarded as a near-universal phenomenon. According to Straus, under what societal conditions is violence most likely to be prevalent?

    c. Define *child abuse*. How many children are estimated to be abused by their parents each year?

    d. What has research revealed concerning the rate of elder abuse?

H. **Globalization: Impacts on the Family.** Changes in the family reflect the changes taking place in the larger society and the world.

1. This section begins with a discussion of the ways in which WWII brought about changes in the American family. Briefly explain how WWII shaped and then reshaped women's role in the family.

    a. What effect did WWII have on the birth rate in America?

b.   What has been the impact of globalization on the American class structure?

III.   STUDENT ACTIVITIES

1.   The text discusses family differences associated with class, race, and ethnicity. Do you feel that your family values independence and individual initiative or respect for authority and obedience? Do the family patterns associated with a particular race correspond to your own family experience with regard to marriage, divorce, and single parenting? Do you agree or disagree with the way in which families of the various racial and ethnic groups are characterized? Why or why not?

2.   During the 1950s, fewer than 1 percent of all marriages in the U.S. ended in divorce. Today, the U.S. has one of the highest rates of divorce. Why do you think divorce is so much more prevalent today? Do you think that married life was more satisfying forty years ago? Do you agree that there were stronger norms favoring marriage forty years ago than there are today? Do you think that couples who cohabit as a "trial marriage" are less likely to divorce later on?

IV.   KEY TERMS

Listed below are some of the key terms that are introduced in Chapter 14. After you have read the chapter in your text and worked through the overview on the preceding pages, test your recall by writing the definitions of the terms in the space provided. You may check your work by referring to the *Key Terms* section at the end of the chapter in your text.

baby boomers _____

_____

cohabitation _____

_____

divorce rate _____

_____

endogamy _____

_____

extended family _____

_____

family _____

_____

international _____

_____

marriage rate _____

_____

monogamy _____

_____

nuclear family _____

_____

V.   TEST QUESTIONS

Multiple-Choice Questions
Choose the correct answer from the choices provided.

1.   Most people choose mates who are from roughly the same social class, age, race, and ethnic group. This practice is referred to as:
   a.   endogamy.
   b.   monogamy.
   c.   polygyny.
   d.   polyandry.

2.   Which of the following is not true of the family in modern society?
   a.   The family is socially constructed within a given culture.
   b.   The family consists of people who identify themselves as being related to one another in some way.
   c.   The family always consists of two parents and dependent children.
   d.   The family differs by race, class, and ethnicity.

3.   Which of the following family forms is the law in the U.S.?
   a.   polygamy
   b.   monogamy
   c.   polygyny
   d.   endogamy

4.   According to functionalist theory, the function of the family is to:
   a.   provide biological reproduction to perpetuate society.
   b.   to socialize children.
   c.   to provide intimacy and social support.
   d.   all of the above

5. Which of the following is not an argument made by conflict theorists concerning the family?
   a. The family serves to reproduce relations of authority and gender inequality.
   b. The social capital children acquire in their families reflects class position and helps to reproduce social stratification.
   c. The family contributes to the social stability of society as a whole.
   d. Women's role in the family is to work without pay at home, entering the paid workforce only when their labor is needed.

6. Industrialization shifted the roles of the family to emphasize:
   a. socialization of children.
   b. emotional fulfillment and consumption.
   c. economic production.
   b. all of the above.

7. Marriages in modern society are:
   a. less stable than in preindustrial society.
   b. more stable than in preindustrial society.
   c. based on economic consideration.
   d. both b and c

8. The marriage rate, the ratio of the number of people who actually marry in a given year compared to the total number of people eligible to marry,
   a. has been declining since the 1960s.
   b. has been increasing since the 1960s.
   c. has remained stable since the 1960s.
   d. has been increasing for whites since the 1960s, while decreasing for other racial and ethnic groups.

9. Which of the following illustrate the effects of globalization?
   a. The baby boom.
   b. Increased demand for upper and middle class men and women with skills and Training in management, administration, and engineering.
   c. An increased need for working class families to depend on two incomes to make ends meet.
   d. all of the above.

10. An extended family is:
    a. composed of an adult couple and their children.
    b. smaller than a nuclear family.
    c. composed of one or more parents, children, and other kin.
    d. one that has "extended" its economic resources.

True/False Questions

For each of the following statements, decide whether the statement is true or false. Write your answer in the space provided.

_____ 1. The meaning of "family" is socially constructed within a particular culture.

_____ 2. People who choose mates from the same social class or age group, for example, are considered to be endogamous.

_____ 3. Today the vast majority of American households can be characterized as nuclear families.

_____ 4. There is little cultural variation in who takes responsibility for child rearing

_____ 5. Monogamy is the most common form of marital arrangement in the United States.

_____ 6. The pursuit of companionship, romantic love, and emotional fulfillment marriage is a feature of human relationships that dates back to ancient times.

_____ 7. The marriage rate in the U.S. has been steadily declining since the 1960s.

_____ 8. The rate of divorce is higher among families without children than it is among families where children are involved.

_____ 9. In American culture, middle and upper class families tend to emphasize independence in their children, whereas working class families are more likely to emphasize respect for authority and obedience.

_____ 10. William Julius Wilson argues that different family patterns between blacks and whites is due, in part, to American society's creation of a permanent black urban underclass.

Matching Exercise

For each of the following terms, identify the correct definition and write the appropriate letter in the space provided.

a.   child abuse
b.   child-minding
c.   cohabitation
d.   domestic violence
e.   marriage
f.   no fault divorce
g.   polyandry
h.   polygamy

i. polygyny
j. serial monogamy

_____ 1. the physical, sexual, or psychological abuse committed by one family member on another.

_____ 2. a culturally approved relationship, usually between two individuals, that provides for a degree of economic cooperation, intimacy, and sexual activity.

_____ 3. a form of marriage in which a man may have multiple wives.

_____ 4. a form of abuse involving sexual and/or physical assaults on children by adult members of their family.

_____ 5. a relatively recent form of divorce that permits couples to divorce purely on the grounds of incompatibility.

_____ 6. the practice of having more than one wife or husband, but only one at a time.

_____ 7. an arrangement in which extended family members and friends cooperate in raising the children of a person who is living in another locale.

_____ 8. a form of marriage in which a person may have more than one spouse at a time.

_____ 9. living together as a married couple without being married.

_____ 10. a form of marriage in which a woman may have multiple husbands.

Completion
Write in the word(s) that best completes each of the following statements. To check your work, refer to the answer key at the end of this study guide.

1. A _____ is sociologically defined as a group of people who identify themselves as being related to one another.

2. The _____ theory of the family emphasizes the way in which the family contributes to maintenance of the larger society through, for example, biological reproduction, socialization of children, and protection of the helpless.

3. According to _____ theory, the family serves to reproduce the relations of authority that exist in the wider society, emphasizing in particular the production of gender inequality.

4. _____ is a form of marriage in which a woman may have multiple husbands.

5. A family consisting of one or two parents and their dependent children is referred to as a _____ family.

6. Global family arrangements in which extended family members or friends cooperate in raising the children of a person living in another locale is referred to as _____.

7. In most societies, marriages tend to be _____, involving mates who come from the same kinship group, social category, or other social group.

8. Many young families had to postpone having children during WWII, leading to a _____ _____ in the decade after World War II in which an unusually large number of children were born.

9. _____, having only one spouse at time, is the law in the United states.

10. A situation in which a couple lives together in a kind of "trial marriage" is referred to as _____.

CHAPTER 15

WORK AND ECONOMIC LIFE

I.   LEARNING OBJECTIVES

1. To become familiar with the organization of work in industrial society, including issues of alienation, productivity, labor market stratification, unionization.
2. To become familiar with the differences between the capitalist, socialist, and industrial-democratic political economic systems.
3. To consider the organization of work in postindustrial society.
4. To understand the effect of globalization on work and economic life in the United States and throughout the world.

II.   CHAPTER OVERVIEW

In this chapter, you are introduced to the work and economic life in the United States and the world. The chapter begins by exploring the birth and development of modern industrial society, from the factory system to the modern corporation.

A.   **What Do Sociologists Mean By 'Work'?** We all have our own understanding of the concept of 'work'. For sociologists, however, 'work' has a very far-reaching meaning. In this section you are introduced to some of the concepts that organize sociological thinking about work and the economy.

    1.   Define the term *work* as used by sociologists.

        a.   What activities are included within this definition of work? What types of activities are excluded?

        b.   How does this definition of work differ from our common-sense understanding of work?

    2.   Work falls into three broad categories: formal economy, underground economy, and unpaid labor.

a. List below the types of work activities that are included within each category.

Formal economy: _____

_____

Underground economy: _____

_____

Unpaid labor: _____

_____

b. What distinquishes work in the informal economy from work in the formal economy?

B. **The Organization of Work in Industrial Society.** In this section, you are introduced to the birth of industrial society, the modern factory system, and the experience of workers.

1. In Chapter 4, *industrial society* was defined as a society in which subsistence is based on the mechanized production of goods in factories. How did the modern factory system differ from earlier forms of economic organization?

a. Briefly explain how factory work contributed to the creation of a class society?

2. The working conditions in nineteenth century factories reflected the living conditions of industrial society. Describe the working conditions in the factories and the experience of factory workers.

a. According to Karl Marx, factory workers under industrial capitalism suffered from *alienation*. Define *alienation*.

b.   List the four ways workers are alienated, and give an example illustrating how each source of alienation occurs in the workplace.

          <u>Alienation</u>   <u>Example</u>

_____   _____

_____   _____

_____   _____

_____   _____

c.   Your text mentions two shortcomings to Marx's theory of alienation. What are they?

(1)

(2)

3.   What were the two principle objectives of the modern industrial factory?

a.   Define *Fordism*, and define and describe Henry Ford's system of *mass production*.

b.   Define *scientific management* as conceived by Frederick Taylor. What was Taylor's main goal?

c.   Define *deskilling*, and explain how work became deskilled with scientific management.

4.   Define the terms *labor market* and *dual labor market*.

194

a. Use the chart below to list the two strata of the dual labor market, the types of jobs found in each, and which group(s) of people fill those occupations.

Strata   Types of occupations   Groups

5. Although the informal economy includes work activities that evade regulation governmental institutions, it has become an integral part of the modern industrial-capitalist economy. Briefly explain why this is so.

a. How does the informal economy support the formal economy?

6. Labor unions have played an important part in the organization of work in the U.S. What are *labor unions*, and what are some of the ways they support workers?

a. Briefly discuss the development and primary concerns of the first American unions.

b. How has union membership and participation changed since the 1950s, and how are the changes explained?

c. What changes have unions made to keep pace with a growing global economy?

7. The *corporation* is a major organizational form in industrial society. Define and briefly characterize the following forms of power concentration in the modern corporation, and briefly describe their place in industrial society.

a.   Corporate power can become concentrated in a number of ways. Define the following corporate forms, and briefly describe their place in industrial society.

monopoly: _____
_____
_____

oligopoly: _____
_____
_____

interlocking directorates: _____
_____
_____

conglomerate: _____
_____
_____

b.   What are *transnational corporations (TNC)*, and why are they important in a global economy? Give an example of a transnational corporation.

c.   What concerns arise about the people and countries in which transnational corporations operate?

C.   **Politics and the Economy.** In this section, you will be introduced to the three political economic systems: capitalist, socialist, and industrial democratic.

1.   Describe the *capitalist political-economic system*.

a.   How do capitalist enterprises keep costs down? What are some of the consequences of their cost-saving strategies?

b.   What is the work ethic underlying capitalist systems?

2.   Describe the *socialist political-economic system*.

       a.   What is the work ethic underlying socialist systems?

       b.   How do socialist political-economic systems differ from capitalist systems?

       c.   List some of the drawbacks to socialist systems and some of the ways in which they have been successful.

3.   Describe *industrial democracy*, and explain how it holds a middle ground between capitalist and socialist systems.

       a.   List some of the countries that can be characterized as industrial democratic.

       b.   List some of the ways in which industrial democratic countries provide for their citizens?

D.   **Postindustrial Society.**

    1.   In 1973, Daniel Bell argued that we are entering a *postindustrial society*. How does Bell characterize *postindustrial society*?

    2.   Scholars depict postindustrial society in one of two ways. Please explain.

3. In 1964, Marshall McLuhan wrote that we are living in a "global village." Briefly explain what McLuhan means by this.

4. The "information revolution" will impact the organization of work and economic life in postindustrial society in many ways. One way is through the *automation* of manufacturing. Define *automation*, and give an example illustrating how the manufacturing process has become automated.

    a. What is the experience of workers in highly automated factories as compared to non-automated factories?

    b. What are the two possible effects of automation on the American workforce?

5. One result of automation is increased *flexibility* in production. How does the *post-Fordist* form of industrial organization differ from the Fordist form of industrial society?

    a. What does it mean to say that production is *vertically-integrated*?

6. Define *subcontracting*, and explain how it contributes to the postindustrial form of flexible organization and benefits business. What are the consequences of subcontracting for workers?

7. Use the chart below to identify and define the three different sectors of the economy. Give examples of the types of jobs included and the percent of the workforce within each sector.

	Sector	Definition	Types of jobs	Percent
(1)				
(2)				
(3)				

8. What is a *symbolic analyst*? (Be sure to note the distinction between symbolic analysts and workers who use high-technology equipment.)

9. The "information revolution" has also reduced the need for workers to be in the same physical location as the company that employs them. This is accomplished by means of the *virtual workplace*. What is a *virtual workplace*?

   a. What is *telecommuting*, and what technologies make telecommuting possible? Give an example of a company that utilizes these business technologies.

   b. How are telecommuting and the virtual workplace changing the nature of work in the U.S.?

10. How does the transition to postindustrial society threaten the American standard of living?

E. **Globalization: Toward a Single World Economy?**

1. Increased globalization has drawn the world closer to a unified global economic system. Briefly describe how the transition from industrial society to postindustrial society has contributed to the emergence of a unified global economic system.

2.	What are the consequences of increased globalization with regard to the market for labor?

	a.	What is the *global wage*? What types of occupations are seeing the emergence of the global wage?

3.	Why are some global industries beginning to relocate to industrial countries, despite lower wages elsewhere around the world?

III.	STUDENT ACTIVITIES

1.	Scholars typically depict postindustrial society in one of two ways: as a prosperous high-tech utopia where electronic gadgetry frees people from alienating labor, or as an increasingly stratified society. Which characterization of the emerging postindustrial society do you think is more accurate? Or, will postindustrial society involve a combination of the two? Do you think that computer technology will give more power to ordinary citizens? Or, will it enable business and government to exert greater control over citizens?

2.	Your text mentions that one of the key issues facing businesses, workers, and policy makers today is the challenge of retaining and creating jobs in a unified global economy. Given what you have learned about the effects of a global labor market on the organization of work and economic life, what can businesses, workers, and policy makers do to retain and create jobs in postindustrial society? What do you think about the emergence of a global wage? The increase in tertiary or service sector jobs? The increase in jobs that require symbolic analysts? Do you think that a move toward an industrial democratic political-economic system might reduce some of the problems facing postindustrial society?

3.	According to Karl Marx, workers experience four forms of estrangement or alienation from the capitalist mode of production: estrangement from the products of one's labor, the labor process, one's co-workers, and from one's own human nature. Do you think Marx's ideas are relevant today? Give an example of a job that is alienating. What steps can be taken to lower alienation? Do you think high-technology can reduce alienation? Or, will it lead to increased alienation?

IV.   KEY TERMS

Listed below are some of the key terms that are introduced in Chapter 15. After you have read the chapter in your text and worked through the overview on the preceding pages, test your recall by writing the definitions of the terms in the space provided. You may check your work by referring to the *Key Terms* section at the end of the chapter in your text.

alienation _____

_____

collective _____

_____

corporation_____

_____

deskilling _____

_____

dual labor market _____

_____

global wage _____

_____

informal economy_____

_____

information float_____

_____

monopoly _____

_____

oligopoly _____

_____

V.   TEST QUESTIONS

Multiple-Choice Questions
Choose the correct answer from the choices provided.

1.   The primary sector does not include:
    a.   restaurant work.
    b.   mining.
    c.   agriculture.
    d.   fishing.

2. Fordism refers to:
   a. scientific management.
   b. automation.
   c. mass production.
   d. redesigning worker tasks.

3. Which of the following believed that workers under industrial capitalism suffered from a condition of alienation?
   a. Frederick W. Taylor
   b. Henry Ford
   c. Daniel Bell
   d. Karl Marx

4. The secondary labor market is filled primarily by:
   a. immigrants, females, and nonwhites.
   b. white males.
   c. black females.
   d. white males and females with a college education.

5. The informal economy generally does not include:
   a. undocumented immigrants.
   b. garage sales.
   c. drug dealing.
   d. sales clerks.

6. Labor union membership is:
   a. growing among public sector employees.
   b. growing among private sector employees.
   c. growing among both public and private sector employees.
   d. declining among both public and private sector employees.

7. The principal organizational form in industrial society is the:
   a. conglomerate.
   b. oligopoly.
   c. corporation.
   d. interlocking directorate.

8. An economic system that seeks some controls over business, along with public provision of basic social services, is:
   a. socialist.
   b. capitalist.
   c. industrial democratic.
   d. postindustrial.

9. Which of the following is emphasized in postindustrial society?
   a. efficiency and productivity
   b. knowledge, information, and services
   c. increased standardization
   d. mass production of goods

10. Which of the follow is not a result of the "information revolution"?
    a. increased reliance on human labor
    b. automation of manufacturing
    c. increased flexibility in the production process
    d. subcontracting

True/False Questions
For each of the following statements, decide whether the statement is true or false. Write your answer in the space provided.

_____ 1. For Marx, alienation mainly refers to the relationship of workers to factory owners and managers.

_____ 2. Research suggests that worker control over the labor process might reduce alienation.

_____ 3. One of the principal objectives of Fordism and Taylorism was to increase productivity.

_____ 4. Scientific management increased the need for specialized skills and training.

_____ 5. The primary labor market includes jobs that are disproportionately filled by native-born white males.

_____ 6. The informal economy provides an important source of work for low-income people.

_____ 7. The U.S. judicial system has always supported the efforts of unionized workers to improve their working lives, including strikes.

_____ 8. Monopolies and oligopolies are two ways in which corporate power is more equitably distributed among various firms within a particular industry.

_____ 9. Capitalist systems are based on an individualist work ethnic.

_____ 10. According to Daniel Bell, postindustrial society is one in which wealth is based on knowledge, information, and the provision of services.

Matching Exercise

For each of the following terms, identify the correct definition and write the appropriate letter in the space provided.

a. automation
b. collectivist orientation
c. Fordism
d. industrial democracy
e. informal economy
f. labor market
g. primary labor market
h. secondary labor market
i. scientific management
j. socialism

_____ 1. consists of jobs that are reasonably secure, provide good pay and benefits, and hold the promise of career advancement.

_____ 2. a political-economic system in which the production and distribution of goods and services is pursued for the common good.

_____ 3. all people who are seeking to sell their labor to others for a wage or salary.

_____ 4. income-generating activities that escape regulation by governmental agencies and institutions.

_____ 5. the replacement of human labor by machines in the process of manufacturing.

_____ 6. the large-scale, highly standardized mass-production of identical commodities on a mechanical assembly line.

_____ 7. a political-economic system that seeks some democratic controls over business, along with the public provision of basic social services.

_____ 8. the belief that members of society should assume responsibility for one another's welfare.

_____ 9. the application of engineering rules to reorganize the actions of the workers themselves (sometimes called Taylorism after its founder).

_____ 10. a labor market that includes unstable jobs with little job security, low pay and few benefits, and little likelihood of career advancement.

Completion

Write in the word(s) that best completes each of the following statements. To check your work, refer to the answer key at the end of this study guide.

1. _____ is a political-economic system characterized by the market allocation of goods and services, production for private profit, and private ownership of the means of production.

2. A society in which subsistence is based on the mechanized production of goods in factories is called _____ society.

3. The emergence of _____ contributed to the creation of a class society and led to the rapid growth of cities.

4. Early production processes in which workers labor independently on items of their own design, using their own tools, and working at their own pace is known as _____ production.

5. While the organization of work in industrial society is highly standardized and inflexible, the organization of work in postindustrial is characterized by _____ forms of industrial organization that emphasize flexibility.

6. _____ are enormous corporations comprised of numerous subsidiaries, often consisting of unrelated business enterprises.

7. In the dual labor market, the _____ labor market consists of jobs that are reasonably secure, provide good pay and benefits, and hold the promise of advancement; whereas _____ labor market jobs are unstable, low-paying, and offer little likelihood of advancement.

8. "Traveling" from home to work electronically is referred to as _____ .

9. The _____ sector is the principal economic sector in postindustrial society, accounting for 73 percent of the American workforce.

10. While Taylor's scientific management sought to reorganize the labor process to make it as efficient as possible, work became _____ , robbing workers of any discretion in their work.

CHAPTER 16

EDUCATION

I.   LEARNING OBJECTIVES

1.   To understand how the role and importance of education has changed in the course of American history.
2.   To become familiar with some of the key terms and concepts that organize sociological thinking about education.
3.   To become familiar with the functionalist, social conflict, and symbolic interactionist theories of education.
4.   To understand the relationship between education and issues of equality.
5.   To become familiar with current issues in U.S. education.
6.   To understand the role of education in a globalized world.

II.   CHAPTER OVERVIEW

In this chapter, you are introduced to the role of education in modern society, particularly how education contributes to social stratification and inequality.

A.   **Education and the Global Marketplace.** This section begins by describing the growing public concern about the quality of education in America. After exploring some of the reasons this concern arises, some of the key terms that organize sociological thinking about education are introduced.

   1.   Why is there growing public concern about education in America?

   2.   Define *education*.

      a.   Define *formal education*, and explain its relationship to education that occurs informally.

      b.   Define *mass education*. What questions are raised by the existence of mass education?

B.	**A Crisis In U.S. Education.** Is education in the United States in crisis? In this section, you will explore several concerns that have been expressed over education in the United States.

1.	One concern is that U.S. students' test scores on standardized tests are declining. Briefly explain the reason behind this concern. What has the National Assessment of Educational Progress (NAEP) revealed about the educational achievement of U.S. students?

2.	What problems arise when comparing U.S. students' achievement with the achievement of students in other countries?

3.	Briefly explain why racial and ethnic segregation is increasing in U.S. schools.

4.	Media reports of violence, weaponry, and rape in schools have increased in recent years. How accurate are these reports?

C.	**Education, industrialization, and the "Credential Society."** In this section, you are introduced to the history of education in the U.S. and how the role of education has changed as society has changed.

1.	Briefly describe the emergence and purpose of the first educational institutions in the U.S.

2.	Industrialization increased the need for *literacy*. Define *literacy*, and explain why it became important with industrialization.

3.	Define and describe the emergence of *public education*.

4.   What is a *credential society*, and what purpose does the possession of a credential serve?

D.   **Theories of Education.** This section introduces you to three sociological theories of education: functionalist, social conflict, and symbolic interactionist.

1.   According to Emile Durkheim, the founder of functionalist theory, modern society presents a problem for creating *social solidarity*. Define *social solidarity*, and briefly explain the problem identified by Durkheim.

a.   How does education address this problem?

b.   Briefly describe how contemporary functionalist theorists view the function of education.

c.   Functionalist theories of education draw on the work of Robert Merton to distinguish between the *manifest* and *latent* functions of education. Use the chart below to define, and give an example of the manifest and latent functions of education.

	Definition	Example
Manifest functions		
Latent functions		

d.   What is the primary critique of functionalist theory of education?

2.   Conflict theories of education emphasize the ways in which education contributes to social inequality. According to this view, how do schools and other educational institutions perpetuate social inequality?

a.   Conflict theorists argue that educational opportunities differ by race, class, and ethnicity. How so?

b.   Conflict theorists also argue that schools socialize children into culturally-determined gender roles. Recalling Critical Thinking Box 16.1 concerning students' performance in science and math, briefly explain how this relates to gender socialization.

c.   What is the primary critique of social conflict theories of education?

3.   What is the main focus of symbolic interactionist theories of education?

a.   What was the primary concern of the study conducted by Rosenthal and Jacobson? What did the researchers conclude about classroom labeling?

b.   Researcher Paul Willis conducted a similar study of classroom labeling. Briefly describe Willis's study, and give the study's main findings.

E.   **Education and Social Equality.** The purpose of this section is to introduce you to the ways in which educational opportunities differ by race, ethnicity, social class, and gender.

1.   *Bilingual education* is one way in which educational institutions have attempted to meet students' educational needs. What is *bilingual education*?

a.   What percentage of U.S. students aged 5-17 do not speak English very well or come from non-English speaking homes?

b.   Although bilingual education has been federally mandated since 1968, it continues to be a strongly debated issue. What are the arguments in favor and against the provision of bilingual education?

Argument in favor of bilingual education: _____

_____

_____

Argument against bilingual education: _____

_____

_____

    c.   Briefly describe two other difficulties that can arise for students from culturally diverse backgrounds.

        (1)

        (2)

2.   Define *school segregation*, and briefly describe its relationship to slavery in the U.S..

    a.   What effect did the 1896 <u>Plessy vs. Ferguson</u> U.S. Supreme court decision have on school segregation?

    b.   What U.S. Supreme Court decision reversed the Court's earlier standing on school segregation? Briefly describe how the public responded to the Court's ruling.

    c.   Define *de facto segregation*, explain how it occurs.

    d.   What steps have the courts taken to overcome racial segregation?

    e.   Why are Asian Americans and American Indians an exception with respect to minority school segregation?

3.   School funding is another issue that can limit educational opportunities for some students. Briefly describe how school funding can vary by states and between different school districts within the same state.

   a.   What was the average amount spent per pupil in the U.S. in 1994-95?

   b.   Describe the situation faced by many urban schools?

4.   Why is it so difficult to determine the effect of race, class, and ethnicity on school achievement?

   a.   Briefly explain the primary focus and findings of James Coleman's study of educational inequality. Why were Coleman's findings so controversial?

   b.   What has sociological research revealed about the impact that school can have on student performance?

   c.   Among children who have lived in poverty for at least a year, what percent have completed high school? What percent have completed high school who have never lived in poverty?

   d.   Among the poorest fourth of young adults aged 18-24, what percent completed a college degree by age 24? Among the wealthiest fourth, what percent completed a college degree by age 24 (Table 16.3)?

   e.   Compare the 1992 high school completion rates for people between the ages of 18 and 24 for whites, Asian-Americans, African Americans, American Indians, and Latinos (Figure 16.4).

F.   **Current Issues in U.S. Education.**   This section explores some of the issues that education in the U.S. must face as we enter the 21st century.

1.   Define *functional literacy*.

2.   In 1993, the U.S. Department of Education conducted a study of functional literacy in the U.S, testing 13,600 adults for various skills and knowledge. According to the study:

    a.   What percent of American adults fell into the lowest literacy category? Describe this level of literacy.

    b.   What percent of American adults fell into the 2nd lowest proficiency level? Describe this level of literacy.

    c.   What percent of the American adult population was found to have the highest literacy level?

    d.   What did the study report concerning the relationship between literacy and socioeconomic status (SES)?

3.   What is *Head Start*?

    a.   What population is served by Head Start programs? What percent of poor 4-year-olds are reached by Head Start programs?

    b.   What has been concluded about the performance of children who have participated in Head Start and similar programs as compared to children who have not attended such programs?

4.   Briefly explain why financing education is so controversial. Include in your answer a discussion of the controversy over using property taxes to finance education.

5.   What are *school choice plans*?

        a.   What are the arguments in favor and against school choice plans?

6.   Define the practice of *tracking*, and explain how tracking can create a stratified
        school.

7.   What are *magnet schools*?

        a.   What population are magnet schools designed to reach? How effective are
                magnet schools in meeting the educational needs of students?

G.   **Globalization and Education.**   This section introduces you to the ways in which
        globalization is changing education in the U.S. and throughout the world.

        1.   There is a marked disparity in between the U.S. and other industrial societies in the
                number of students who graduate from high school.   What percent of U.S.
                students complete high school? What percent of students complete high school in
                Denmark, Finland, and Germany? In Japan, France, and Swizerland?

                a.   The U.S. spends more on education than many other industrial countries,
                        yet U.S. students spend less time in school. Compare the number of days
                        per year U.S. students spend in school to students in Germany and Japan.

                b.   Briefly explain how a global labor market is making new demands on
                        education.

c. How does the U.S. compare to other industrialized countries with regard to providing educational programs to develop computer literacy?

d. Educational institutions are responding to the demands of increased globalization. Briefly explain how the skills and abilities required in a global marketplace are changing high school and college curricula in the United States.

III. STUDENT ACTIVITIES

1. Globalization requires a major rethinking in our approach to education, including a greater emphsis on economics, political geography, and international relations. What other steps can educational institutions take to prepare students for a global labor market? Although school funding in the U.S. is often limited, what can schools do to enhance their educational programs to include computer training, international education, language, global economics, and so forth? What is the responsibility of families, government, and religious organizations in preparing citizens to participate in a global society?

2. If our educational systems reinforce existing patterns of social inequality, what steps can be taken to change it? What characteristics of the school system contribute to maintenance of social inequality? In the classroom? In the relationship between teachers and students from diverse backgrounds? In the availability of computer technology? In the educational programs that are offered? In the availability of school funding?

IV. KEY TERMS

Listed below are some of the key terms that are introduced in Chapter 16. After you have read the chapter in your text and worked through the overview on the preceding pages, test your recall by writing the definitions of the terms in the space provided. You may check your work by referring to the *Key Terms* section at the end of the chapter in your text.

bilingual education _____

_____

credential society _____

_____

de facto segregation _____

_____

education _____

_____

formal education _____

_____

literacy _____

_____

mass education _____

_____

public education _____

_____

school segregation _____

_____

tracking _____

_____

V.   TEST QUESTIONS

Multiple-Choice Questions
Choose the correct answer from the choices provided.

1.   Which of the following is not a latent function of education?
     a.   teaching children how to read
     b.   teaching children to follow rules
     c.   teaching children to show respect for authority
     d.   preparing children for their adult roles

2.   Which of the following researchers found that British boys from working class families were systematically labeled as low academic achievers and were taught to think of themselves as only capable of having working class jobs?
     a.   Rosenthal and Jacobson
     b.   Paul Willis
     c.   Emile Durkheim
     d.   James Coleman

3.   In its 1954 Brown vs. Board of Education decision, the U.S. Supreme Court:
     a.   upheld the states' rights to segregate schooling.
     b.   ruled that segregated public schools were unconstitutional.
     c.   upheld the states' rights to allow de facto segregation.
     d.   initiated school busing programs to achieve racial integration in public schools.

4.   What percent of all U.S. students graduate from high school?
      a.   25%
      b.   50%
      c.   75%
      d.   90%

5.   A credential society:
      a.   makes it easier for people to get jobs without a high school or college degree.
      b.   places greater emphasis on one's skills and knowledge than on one's level of schooling.
      c.   makes one's qualifications for a particular job dependent on the possession of a certifying credential of education.
      d.   none of the above.

6.   According to functionalist theory, education:
      a.   promotes social solidarity.
      b.   allocates members of society into their appropriate adult roles.
      c.   teaches children to follow rules and show respect for authority.
      d.   all of the above.

7.   Rosenthal and Jacobson's study of classroom interactions among teachers and students found that:
      a.   students who were labeled as "exceptional" performed no better or worse than their peers.
      b.   students who were labeled as "exceptional" outperformed their peers.
      c.   teachers treated students labeled as "exceptional" no differently than any other students.
      d.   teachers gave greater attention to students who were not labeled as "exceptional" in an effort to help them perform better.

8.   Social conflict theorists argue that the primary function of schools in American society is to:
      a.   reduce class-based inequalities by giving students skills and training that are necessary in modern society.
      b.   teach students to hold academic aspirations that will take them beyond the social class of their parents.
      c.   reinforce students' class identification
      d.   reinforce the values necessary to produce a disciplined and competent workforce.

9. Symbolic interactionist research has found that:
   a. classroom labeling occurs only in American culture.
   b. white males often receive class grades higher than their actual test scores.
   c. older students' self-image was more flexible than younger students and, therefore, exhibited the greatest improvement in performance when labeled "exceptional."
   d. labeling of students as exceptional often results in a self-fulfilling prophecy where students begin to see themselves as more intelligent than their peers.

10. Between 1986 and 1990, people who did not finish high school averaged what percent less income than people who completed high school?
    a. 25%
    b. 30%
    c. 45%
    d. 50%

True/False Questions
For each of the following statements, decide whether the statement is true or false. Write your answer in the space provided.

_____ 1. Mass education is consistent with the democratic ideals that are professed in most industrial societies.

_____ 2. The first educational institutions in the U.S. emerged with industrialization in the late 18th century.

_____ 3. The transmission of general knowledge is a manifest function of education.

_____ 4. Criticisms of existing institutions and demands for radical change often come from the most highly educated groups in society.

_____ 5. Conflict theories of education argue that schools socialize members of the working class to accept their class position.

_____ 6. Symbolic interactionist theories of education focus on the ways in which students are labeled as high or low achievers, and how those labels reinforce differences among students.

_____ 7. James Coleman's study of student performance in school found that students' social class background had little to do with overall school achievement.

_____ 8. School segregation is a long-standing problem that persists today.

9. U.S. students place near the top on standardized test scores in mathematics and science as compared to other industrialized nations.

10. Rosenthal and Jacobson's study of classroom interactions between teachers and students found that students falsely labeled as "exceptional" outperformed their peers.

Matching Exercise
For each of the following terms, identify the correct definition and write the appropriate letter in the space provided.

a.   Functional literacy
b.   Head Start
c.   Latent functions
d.   Magnet schools
e   Manifest functions
f.   Private schools
g.   School busing
h.   School choice plans
i.   School segregation
j   Social solidarity

1. the education of racial minorities in schools that are geographically separated from those attended by whites and other ethnic groups.

2. schools that are run by privately-employed educators and paid for out of students' fees and tuition.

3. a federally funded program in which enriched preschool environments are created for lower-income children.

4. schools that seek to attract students by offering specialized, high-quality programs in math, science, arts, humanities or other subjects.

5. the ability to read and write at a level sufficient for accomplishing everyday practical needs.

6. programs in which the government provides families with educational certificates or "vouchers" that can be redeemed for tuition payments at any private or parochial school.

7. the transmission of general knowledge, skills, and other intended functions of education.

_____ 8. a court-ordered program to achieve racial integration by sending public school students to schools other than those they would normally attend.

_____ 9. bonds that unite the members of a social group.

_____ 10. teaching students to govern their lives by time, to sit at desks, to follow rules, to show respect for authority, and other unintended functions of education.

Completion

Write in the word(s) that best completes each of the following statements. To check your work, refer to the answer key at the end of this study guide.

1. _____ serves to transmit knowledge, information, and skills, and to socialize children into the norms and values of society.

2. _____ theories of education focus on the ways in which teachers' perceptions of students and students' self-perceptions help create a self-fulfilling prophecy in which students conform to their teachers' expectations.

3. _____ segregation is due, in part, to segregated residential patterns and to the decision by many white parents to send their children to private schools.

4. _____ theories of education argue that education helps to socialize members of society into the norms and values necessary to promote social solidarity.

5. _____ education became widespread throughout the world with the advent of industrial society.

6. Industrialization vastly increased the need for _____, the ability to read and write at a basic level.

7. _____ theories of education focus on the way in which schools socialize members of the working class to accept their class position.

8. _____ education, offering instruction in a non-English language as well as English, is way in which educational institutions have attempted to meet the challenges of cultural diversity in schools.

9. In its 1954 Brown vs. the Board of Education decision, the U.S. Supreme Court ruled that _____ public schools were unconstitutional.

10. _____ literacy is the ability to read and write at a level sufficient for accomplishing everyday practical needs.

CHAPTER 17

RELIGION

I. LEARNING OBJECTIVES

1. To understand how sociologists think about religion and the ways in which sociologists have classified different religions.
2. To become familiar with three primary types of religious organization: church, sect, and cult.
3. To become familiar with the theoretical perspectives on religion and the changing role of religion in modern society.
4. To explore some of the major world religions.
5. To understand the part gender plays in religion.
6. To become familiar with religion in the United States.
7. To explore the global significance of religion.

II. CHAPTER OVERVIEW

The purpose of this chapter is to introduce the sociological study of religion and the role of religion in modern society.

A. **The Sociological Study of Religion.** In this section you are introduced to the ways in which sociologists think about and study religion.

    1. What is the sociological definition of *religion*?

        a. List the three key elements to the sociological definition of religion.

            (1)

            (2)

            (3)

    2. There are several ways that sociologists have classified different religions: animistic, theistic, and non-theistic.

        a. Define *animistic religion.*

            (1)   Where are animistic religions commonly found?

b.   Define *theistic religion.*

      (1)   Define and compare *polytheism* and *monotheism.*

c.   Define *non-theistic religion.*

      (1)   Give an example of a world religion that is classified as non-theistic?

3.   Your text mentions four principles that guide the sociological study of religion. List and give a brief explanation of each.

Principle	Explanation
a.	
b.	
c.	
d.	

4.   List three of the primary concerns or foci of the sociological study of religion.

B.   **Types of Religious Organizations.** In this section you are introduced to the principal kinds of religious organizations, including church, sect, and cult.

1.   Define *church.*

    a.   Sociologically speaking, what does it mean to say that churches are <u>well-integrated</u>?

    b.   List and define the two forms that churches can take.

        (1)

        (2)

2.   Define *sect*.

      a.   List some of the ways in which sects are distinguished from churches.

      b.   Briefly describe what happens when successful sects grow in size, increasing their appeal to marginal members of society.

3.   Define *cult*.

      a.   Briefly describe some of the distinguishing characteristics of cults, and explain how cults originate.

      b.   When do cults emerge and flourish? Give an example of the emergence of a cult in modern society.

C.   **Theoretical Perspectives on Religion.**   This section reviews the major theoretical perspectives on religion.

    1.   Briefly explain why sociologists now focus on religious pluralism rather than religious domination.

    2.   What is the primary focus of the classical view of religion, and what are the names of the researchers with whom the classical view is associated?

      a.   Define *secularization*, and explain the threat it poses for religion.

b. What does Peter Berger mean when he describes religion as a "sacred canopy"?

3. What is the name of Emile Durkheim's influential study of religion?

a. Describe the culture Durkheim based his theories on?

b. The aborigines in Durkheim's study divided their world into two parts. List and define the two worlds below.

(1)

(2)

c. What did Durkheim conclude concerning the social function of the "realm of the sacred"?

d. What did Durkheim see as the solution to the increased secularization of modern industrial society?

e. What are the two fundamental critiques of Durkheim's theory of religion?

4. According the Karl Marx, how does religion maintain inequality in capitalist society?

a. In Marx's view, how is religion a form of alienation?

b. According to Marx, what is the social function of religion? How do Marx's ideas concerning the function of religion compare to Durkheim's?

c.   What are two critiques of Marx's theory of religion?

5.   The study of religion was a major focus of Max Weber's work.   What was Weber's primary research interest?

    a.   What did Weber conclude concerning the relationship between Protestant beliefs and capitalism?

    b.   What is the name of Weber's famous study of religion?

    c.   Briefly explain how, according to Weber, Protestant beliefs provided fertile ground for capitalism to flourish.

    d.   What did Weber mean when he said that modern society would become an "iron cage" without religion?

    e.   What are the two fundamental critiques of Weber's theory of religion?

6.   During the twentieth century, many American sociologists became interested in exploring the importance of religion in the U.S.

    a.   According to Talcott Parsons, what was the primary function of religion?

    b.   How does Parsons' theory of religion respond to the secularization hypothesis that religion is dying in modern society?

     c.   What is *civil religion*, as conceived by Robert Bellah? Give an example illustrating civil religion in modern society.

7.   What is the main thesis of the *religious economy* approach to religion?

     a.   How does the religious economy approach challenge classical theories of religion?

     b.   What are the two reasons competition between religions increases the level of religious involvement in the U.S.?

           (1)

           (2)

     c.   According to Roger Finke and Rodney Stark, what makes a religious group successful?

     d.   What four criticisms are raised with regard to the religious economy approach?

           (1)

           (2)

           (3)

           (4)

D.   **World Religions.** The purpose of this section is to introduce you to the key aspects of six of the major world religions.

     1.   Use the chart below to list the six world religions, the approximate number of followers of each, whether their belief systems are based on animism, polytheism, monotheism, or non-theism, and where the religion predominates.

	Religion	Followers	Classification	Where
a.				
b.				
c.				
d.				
e.				
f.				

E.   **Religion and Gender.** The purpose of this section is to introduce you to the role of gender in religion, particularly women's role in religion.

1.   Many of the world religions emphasize male superiority and exclude women from positions of power. What is the sociological explanation for this?

   a.   Give an example from the Bible that lends support to men's superiority over women or to women's exclusion from positions of theological power.

   b.   What steps have women taken to liberalize theological teachings concerning women's role in religion, particularly within Judaism and Protestantism?

F.   **Religion in the United States**

1.   As your text points out, Americans are a religious people. What have public opinion polls reported concerning the religiosity of Americans?

   a.   According to Wade Clark Roof, why are baby boomers returning to religion?

226

2. What have sociologists concluded concerning trends in religious affiliation in the U.S.?

    a. What is one reason for increased religious affiliation in the U.S.?

    b. There are over 1,500 distinct religions in the U.S. Which religion has the greatest affiliation?

    c. Wade Clark Roof and William McKinney distinguished several groupings of Protestant churches. Use the chart below to list the principal groupings and briefly characterize the socioeconomic status (SES) of their membership.

Groups	SES
(1)	
(2)	
(3)	
(4)	

    d. Why has membership in conservative Protestant churches increased while membership in liberal and moderate Protestant churches has declined?

    e. Why have the number of Jews declined in recent years?

    f. With regard to social and political liberalism and conservatism, which group has been found to be most liberal on issues of, for example, racial justice and women's rights? Most conservative?

3. According to Phillip Hammond, what are the three principal historical periods during which religion has become *disestablished* in the U.S.? First, define the term *disestablished.* Then, using the chart below, identify the periods by date and the particular historical event(s) that marked periods of disestablishment.

	Date	Historical event(s)
a.		
b.		
c.		

4. How do Roger Finke and Rodney Stark view the process of disestablishment?

5. Define *evangelicalism*, and give an example illustrating this form of religion.

   a. What strategies have evangelical organizations used to mobilized resources to achieve their religious and political objectives?

   b. What are *televangelists*, and how successful are they in reaching American households?

   c. Who are the *fundamentalist* evangelicals? Give an example of an individual or group that represents this form of evangelicalism.

   d. What is the primary concern of fundamentalist evangelical organizations?

G. **Globalization and Religion.** In this section you are introduced to religion as a long-standing global institution.

1. What is *liberation theology*? Give an example illustrating how liberation theology has brought about social or political change.

2. What is *religious nationalism*? Give an example and briefly describe a religious nationalist movement.

    a. How do religious nationalist movements view the relationship between religion, government, and politics?

    b. Why do some scholars see the emergence of religious nationalist movements as a "new Cold War"?

III. STUDENT ACTIVITIES

1. Considering what you have learned about religion and religious organizations, do you think religion promotes change or maintains the status quo? Consider, for example, what you have learned about liberation theology and religious nationalism. Do you believe that religious organizations should be involved in social or political activism?

2. Which view of religion appeals to you? Durkheim's theory about the functions of religion? Marx's theory about religion and inequality? Weber's theory about the relationship between Protestantism and capitalism? Or, do you prefer the religious economy approach? Or do you think that each of the theories offer some insight into religion in modern society?

IV. KEY TERMS

Listed below are some of the key terms that are introduced in Chapter 17. After you have read the chapter in your text and worked through the overview on the preceding pages, test your recall by writing the definitions of the terms in the space provided. You may check your work by referring to the *Key Terms* section at the end of the chapter in your text.

animistic religion _____

_____

civil religion _____

_____

cult _____

_____

monotheism _____

_____

nontheistic religions _____

_____

polytheism _____

_____

religion _____

_____

sect _____

_____

secular _____

_____

totem _____

_____

V.   TEST QUESTIONS

Multiple-Choice Questions
Choose the correct answer from the choices provided.

1.   Sociologists study religion to determine:
   a.   the psychological response of individuals to religion.
   b.   its truth or falsity.
   c.   how religions function as social institutions in society.
   d.   whether a particular belief system is morally good or bad.

2.   Sects:
   a.   are well-integrated with society.
   b.   are allied with the state.
   c.   exists in a high degree of tension with their environment.
   d.   tend to intellectualize religious practices.

3. Whose theory of religion believes that Protestant beliefs provided fertile ground for capitalism to flourish?
   a. Emile Durkheim
   b. Max Weber
   c. Karl Marx
   d. John Calvin

4. The idea that religion is the "opium of the people" is attributed to:
   a. Karl Marx.
   b. Peter Berger.
   c. Emile Durkheim.
   d. Max Weber.

5. According to the classical view, which of the following is not an function of religion?
   a. To maintain inequality in industrial society.
   b. To maintain social solidarity.
   c. To reaffirm society's norms and values.
   d. To bring community together.

6. Secularization refers to:
   a. an increase in social and political power of religious organizations.
   b. an increase in religious beliefs and involvement.
   c. a rise in the influence of religion and a decline in worldly thinking.
   d. a decline in the influence of religion and an increase in worldly thinking.

7. Religious economists argue that:
   a. competition between religious organizations decreases the overall level of religious involvement in modern society.
   b. competition between religious organizations increases the overall level of religious involvement in modern society.
   c. the existence of a religious monopoly will assure the vitality of religion in modern society.
   d. religious pluralism discourages the appeal of religion in modern society.

8. Which of the following religions is polytheistic?
   a. Christianity
   b. Islam
   c. Judaism
   d. Hinduism

9. According to public opinion polls:
   a. a majority of Americans believe in God.
   b. a minority of American believe in God.
   c. the U.S. is one of the least religious of all industrial nations.
   d. few Americans regularly pray.

10. Considering the correlates of religious affiliation, which of the following religious groupings have the highest socioeconomic profile?
   a.   conservative Protestants and Catholics
   b.   liberal Protestants and Catholics
   c.   conservative Protestants and Jews
   d.   liberal Protestants and Jews

True/False Questions
For each of the following statements, decide whether the statement is true or false. Write your answer in the space provided.

_____   1.   Sociologists view religion as a form of culture.

_____   2.   In the study of religion, sociologists are primarily concerned with whether religious beliefs are true or false.

_____   3.   Sects are often at odds with established churches.

_____   4.   Secularization is a rise in worldly thinking and a simultaneous decline in the influence of religion.

_____   5.   Karl Marx believed that state-sponsored "moral education" would substitute for traditional religion in modern society.

_____   6.   Max Weber was especially interested in the relationship between religious beliefs and economic life, particularly the relationship between Protestantism and capitalism.

_____   7.   The American pledge of allegiance, by referring to "one nation under God," is an expression of civil religion.

_____   8.   The religious economy approach argues that religion in modern society is threatened by scientific thinking and the side-by-side coexistence of competing religions.

_____   9.   Religious nationalist movements call for a separation of religion, government, and politics.

_____   10.   Church membership has declined steadily since the United States was founded.

Matching Exercise

For each of the following terms, identify the correct definition and write the appropriate letter in the space provided.

a. church
b. denomination
c. disestablishment
d. evangelicalism
e. liberation theology
f. profane
g. religious economy
h. religious nationalism
i. secularization
j. televangelists

_____ 1. the fusion of strongly-held religious convictions with beliefs about a nation's social and political destiny.

_____ 2. in Durkheim's view, the sphere of mundane, routine, everyday life.

_____ 3. various times in American history when the social and political influence of established religions has been successfully challenged.

_____ 4. a religious organization that exists in a fairly harmonious, well-integrated relationship with the larger society.

_____ 5. a theoretical framework that argues that religions can be fruitfully understood as organizations in competition with one another for adherents.

_____ 6. a religious movement, centered primarily in Latin America, that combines Catholic beliefs, a passion for social justice for the poor, and actions aimed at achieving that passion.

_____ 7. a form of Protestantism characterized by a belief in spiritual rebirth, an emphasis on emotional and personal spiritual piety, and commitment to proselytizing.

_____ 8. a rise in worldly thinking and a simultaneous decline in the influence of religion.

_____ 9. individuals who conduct their ministries over television, reaching a much wider audience than previously possible.

_____ 10. a church that is not formally allied with the state.

Completion
Write in the word(s) that best completes each of the following statements. To check your work, refer to the answer key at the end of this study guide.

1. According to the classical view, religion in modern society is threatened by a long-term process of _____, whereby the challenge of scientific thinking and the coexistence of competing religions will inevitably lead to the demise of religion altogether.

2. The _____ _____ approach argues that secularization and competition among religious groups force religions to work harder to win adherents, thereby strengthening the various groups and countering secularization.

3. _____ has always been one of the most global of all social institutions.

4. _____ religions believe that naturally-occurring phenomena, such as mountains and animals, are possessed of indwelling spirits with supernatural powers.

5. A _____ is a religious organization that exists in a fairly harmonious relationship with the larger society, whereas a _____ is a religion that is unconventional with regard to the larger society.

6. According to Emile Durkheim, the realm of _____ serves an important social function in that it brings the community together, reaffirms its norms and values, and strengthens its social bonds.

7. For Karl Marx, religion is a form of _____, whereby members of a society project an imagined deity the qualities they most esteem in themselves.

8. Robert Bellah argued that some societies possess a _____ _____--beliefs through which they interpret their own histories in light of some conception of ultimate reality.

9. Judaism and Christianity are two world religions that adhere to a _____ belief in a single God.

10. According to Phillip Hammond, there have been three principal historical periods during which religion has become _____ in the U.S.--that is, where the social and political influence of established religions has been successfully challenged.

CHAPTER 18

MEDICINE AND HEALTH

I.   LEARNING OBJECTIVES

1.   To understand the importance of sociology for medicine and to distinguish between health and medicine.
2.   To understand how illness is socially constructed within a particular culture, and what the social construction of illness means for the doctor-patient relationship and to the medicalization of health.
3.   To become familiar with the medical profession in the United States.
4.   To become familiar with health care in the United States, including inequalities in health care and access to health care, rising costs, and current issues in the provision of health care to Americans.
5.   To understand the impact of globalization on health and medicine.

II.   CHAPTER OVERVIEW

The purpose of this chapter is to introduce you to the sociological study of medicine and health in the United States and as a global concern.

A.   **Introduction: Sociology, Health, and Medicine.** This section will introduce you to the sociology of medicine and will distinguish between health and medicine.

   1.   What about health and health care in the 20th century made sociology important to understanding issues of health and medicine?

         a.   Define *health*.

         b.   Define *medicine*.

         c.   Define *preventive medicine*.

B. **Cultural Definitions of Health and Illness.** In this section, you are introduced to the social construction of illness, including the doctor-patient relationship and the way in which health and illness have become increasingly medicalized.

1. Briefly explain Talcott Parsons' notion of *sick roles*.

   a. Summarize Parsons' three observations on the rights and responsibilities associated with the role of sick person.

      (1)

      (2)

      (3)

2. Illnesses culturally defined as "legitimate" entitle those who contract them to adopt the "sick role." There can be some ambiguity, however, in the social definition of an illness. List some of the disorders that have been difficult to define, and briefly explain the controversy that exists over their legitimacy.

   <u>Disorder</u>   <u>Explanation</u>

   a.

   b.

   c.

3. What is the *medicalization of health and illness*?

   a. Define *hyperactivity*, and explain how it has been redefined through the process of medicalization?

C. **The Medical Profession in the United States.** The medical profession in the United States has changed dramatically since the turn of the century. In this section, you will learn how medicine has become institutionalized in modern society.

1. Briefly characterize the medical profession in the United States prior to the turn of the century and the efforts of the American Medical Association (AMA) to redefine the practice of medicine.

    a. What were the results of Abraham Flexner's 1908 study of medical education? How did his study help to establish the "cultural authority of medicine"?

2. The authoritative relationship between doctor and patient is reproduced in interaction, thus reflecting and reinforcing the authority and gender relations in the larger society. List some of the ways in which this doctor/patient relationship is achieved in interaction.

    (1)

    (2)

    (3)

    a. How is the unequal power between doctor and patient considered by some to be functional for society? How is it considered to be detrimental?

3. Health care occupations have also become institutionalized, reflecting the larger stratification system of society. Use the chart below to list some of the health care occupations that make up the medical stratification system. Identify the groups who fills each occupational category and the social class from which they are recruited.

Medical occupation	Who	Social Class
a.		
b.		
c.		

4. Describe the experience of women physicians, including their medical education and as practicing physicians.

5.   List some of the new health care providers, and briefly describe the gap they fill in the provision of health care. Describe the tensions that exist between new health care providers and physicians.

D.   **Health Care in the United States.** In this section you are introduced to some of the issues central to health care in the U.S., including social inequalities in health and access to health care, and the rising cost of health care.

1.   Define *health care*.

       a.   What does an adequate health care system include?

       b.   How does the U.S. compare to other industrialized nations with regard to meeting the standards of an adequate health care system?

2.   There are significant differences in health and health care by class, race, and ethnicity. What does it mean to say that "health follows the social class curve"?

       a.   Compare the life expectancy of white men and women to that of black men and women.

       b.   Briefly describe some of the lifestyle factors that effect the health of lower class people.

       c.   Your text points out that blacks have a higher mortality rate than whites when they have heart attacks that occur outside of a hospital. Why does this racial difference exist?

d.   Figure 18.4 in your text give self-assessed health by race, age, and family income. What are the socioeconomic characteristics of the people who assess their health as good as compared to people who assess their health as poor?

e.   Inequalities are also found in health-related research.

    (1)   Describe the racial discrimination in the Tuskegee study of illness (see also Chapter 2 in your text).

    (2)   Describe the gender-based discrimination in medical research.

3.   Define *medical care*.

a.   How much did the U.S. spend per person on health care in 1960? How much does the U.S. spend per person on health care today?

b.   The U.S. spends more per person on medical care than any other industrial nation, yet health care in the U.S. is not the most comprehensive system. List the factors that contribute to the rising medical costs in the U.S.

    (1)

    (2)

    (3)

    (4)

c.   The high cost of medical technology has contributed to the rising cost of medical care in the U.S., including technologies that enable *heroic measures*. What are *heroic measures*, and what controversies exist over the use of such measures to preserve life?

d. Define and give an example of *negative euthanasia* and *positive euthanasia*.

e. What are the moral and economic concerns that arise in the debate over euthanasia?

f. The rising cost of physicians' services also contribute to the cost of medical care in the U.S. What factors contribute to the high cost of physicians' services?

g. What was the average after-expense income of all doctors in the U.S. between 1982 and 1992 as compared to the median income of full-time male workers?

h. Briefly explain how cost containment contributes to the rising cost of medical care in the U.S.

i. Define *primary health care*, and explain how it contributes to rising medical costs.

4. In some countries, a *national health service* provides universal access to health care. What is a *national health service*, and which countries provide such services?

5. Describe the *fee-for-service* system of health care that is found in the U.S.

a. What are some of the drawbacks the fee-for-service system of health care?

240

b. How many Americans are estimated to be without any form of health insurance?

6. What are *health maintenance organizations*? Briefly characterize the emergence and growth of health maintenance organizations in the U.S.

7. Although the U.S. does not offer universal health coverage, there are two health care programs that are supported by the government. List and define the government supported health care programs mentioned in your text.

a.

b.

8. In 1992, the Clinton administration promoted a form of health care termed *managed competition*. What is *managed competition*?

a. What concerns have arisen within the insurance industry and medical community over managed competition?

E. **Globalization: Impacts on Health and Medicine.** The purpose of this section is to introduce you to the impacts of globalization on the spread of disease and to the global efforts that have been mounted to combat disease.

1. This section begins by noting that the "spread of disease knows no national boundaries." List some of the diseases that have been spread through contact between different populations.

a. AIDS is one of the most recent examples of the global spread of disease. Why has AIDS spread so rapidly around the world?

241

b.   Who have been the primary carriers of the AIDS virus worldwide?

c.   How many people worldwide are estimated to have full-blown AIDS? How many people are estimated to be infected with the HIV virus?

d.   How is AIDS transmitted?

e.   Why is the impact of disease more acute in the poorer countries of the world?

f.   What steps have been taken globally to prevent and treat such catastrophic illnesses?

III.   STUDENT ACTIVITIES

1.   This chapter has introduced you to the social construction of illness--how, for example, certain illnesses or disorders are defined as legitimate and entitling those who contract them to adopt the role of "sick person."   Consider some of the illnesses or disorders where ambiguity still exists in their social definition--drug and alcohol use, chronic fatigue syndrome, AIDS, and mental illness. Do you agree or disagree that these are legitimate illnesses? What, in your opinion, makes these legitimate or illegitimate illnesses? Do you think people who contract these illnesses are entitled to adopt the "sick role"? Do you think that the managed competition health care system should provide health coverage for these illnesses? Why or why not?

2.   Much controversy exists over the use of euthanasia, especially positive euthanasia --actively killing a severely ill person who would otherwise live, as an act of mercy--or "mercy killings." Do you think that positive euthanasia should be made legal in the United States? What moral or economic concerns do you have concerning the use of euthanasia? Do you think that certain racial or ethnic groups might be more or less likely to make use of euthanasia? What issues arise concerning the graying of America and the legalization of euthanasia?

IV.   KEY TERMS

Listed below are some of the key terms that are introduced in Chapter 18. After you have read the chapter in your text and worked through the overview on the preceding pages, test your recall by writing the definitions of the terms in the space provided. You may check your work by referring to the *Key Terms* section at the end of the chapter in your text.

euthanasia _____

_____

fee-for-service _____

_____

health care _____

_____

health _____

_____

heroic measures _____

_____

managed competition _____

_____

medical care _____

_____

medicalization of health and illness _____

_____

medicine _____

_____

preventive medicine _____

_____

V.   TEST QUESTIONS

Multiple-Choice Questions
Choose the correct answer from the choices provided.

1.   Which of the following is <u>not</u> true regarding the social construction of illness?
        a.   Being healthy is a value in modern society.
        b.   The role of "sick person" includes the right to be excused from social responsibilities.
        c.   Everyone has a right to medical care if they are sick.
        d.   What people view as health and illness is not culturally defined.

2.   As used by sociologists, *health* refers to:
      a.   mental well-being
      b.   physical well-being
      c.   mental, physical, and social well-being
      d.   social well-being only

3.   Which of the following strengthens the power differences between patients and doctors?
      a.   a highly technical medical language.
      b.   the physician's ability to withhold information.
      c.   the fact that most physicians are male.
      d.   all of the above.

4.   In a report to the Carnegie Foundation, Abraham Flexner recommended:
      a.   the relabeling of "high energy" children as hyperactive.
      b.   that the licensing of medical doctors be limited to people trained in university-affiliated medical schools.
      c.   that physicians be allowed to use positive euthanasia when a terminally ill patient requests it.
      d.   that the Clinton Administration adopt a managed competition health care program.

5.   Medicare provides medical insurance for:
      a.   people 65 years and older.
      b.   the disabled, the poor, and those on welfare.
      c.   women and children.
      d.   former members of the armed services and their families.

6.   Which of the following is <u>not</u> true of the health care category of physician?
      a.   Most physicians are white males.
      b.   Most are recruited from the middle and upper middle class.
      c.   Nearly half of all medical students are female.
      d.   Men and women are equally represented in the various medical specialties.

7.   The reorganization of medical education in the early 20th century:
      a.   fostered the belief that the treatment of illness and disease was the only appropriate approach to medicine.
      b.   helped establish the cultural authority of medicine.
      c.   gave certified doctors monopoly control over medical practice.
      d.   all of the above.

8. A 1993 report by the Center for Disease Control found the infant mortality rate for African-Americans to be:
   a. five times the rate for whites.
   b. no different than the mortality rate for whites.
   c. due largely to inadequate prenatal and early childhood health care.
   d. due to biological factors.

9. Which is not true regarding equality of health care in the U.S.?
   a. Blacks have a higher mortality rate than whites when they had a heart attack outside of a hospital.
   b. Racial minorities on average suffer from poorer health than whites.
   c. White men live longer than white women.
   d. White men live longer than black men.

10. Which of the following is not true regarding the epidemic spread of AIDS?
    a. Worldwide, women are much less likely to be infected with the HIV virus than men.
    b. AIDS has been spread around the world primarily by heterosexual businessmen, workers, and tourists.
    c. Worldwide, there are approximately 16 million people infected with the HIV virus.
    d. AIDS in the United States is disproportionately found among homosexual and bisexual men and intravenous drug users.

True/False Questions

For each of the following statements, decide whether the statement is true or false. Write your answer in the space provided.

_____ 1. There are "sick roles" in every society.

_____ 2. According to Talcott Parsons, the unequal power between doctor and patient is dysfunctional for proper health care.

_____ 3. The medicalization of deviance is the transformation of culturally defined deviant behavior into medical problems.

_____ 4. The graying of the American population is not expected to add greatly to the demand for heroic measures.

_____ 5. Negative euthanasia refers to the withdrawing of vital life support systems from a terminally ill person who will die as a direct result.

_____ 6. Nurses are primarily recruited from lower-middle class and working class families.

_____ 7. Female and male doctors earn, on average, the same income.

_____ 8. Class structure in the health care system resembles the class structure in the larger society.

_____ 9. Nearly half of all medical students are female.

_____ 10. The occupational distinctions of doctor, nurse, medical technician, or orderly are socially constructed.

Matching Exercise

For each of the following terms, identify the correct definition and write the appropriate letter in the space provided.

a. health maintenance organizations (HMOs)
b. health
c. hyperactivity
d. Medicaid
e. medicalization of deviance
f. Medicare
g. national health service
h. negative euthanasia
i. positive euthanasia
j. primary care

_____ 1. a federal medical insurance program that provides medical insurance covering hospital costs for all people 65 years and older.

_____ 2. the transformation of culturally-defined deviant behavior into medical problems.

_____ 3. the active killing of a severely ill person who otherwise would live, as an act of mercy.

_____ 4. a federal insurance program that provides health insurance for the disabled, the poor, and those on welfare.

_____ 5. a state of mental, physical, and social well-being.

_____ 6. a health care system that covers everyone in the country regardless of their ability to pay.

_____ 7. medical services that focus on dealing with health problems as they arise rather than after they have become acute.

_____ 8. the withdrawing of vital life support systems from a terminally-ill person who will die as a direct result.

_____ 9. the inability to concentrate for more than a few seconds or moments without being distracted.

_____ 10. groups of doctors and health care specialists who work together and provide services for a set monthly or annual membership fee.

Completion
Write in the word(s) that best completes each of the following statements. To check your work, refer to the answer key at the end of this study guide.

1. _____ refers to a generalized state of wellness, whereas _____ is an institutionalized approach to the prevention of illness.

2. _____ medicine is concerned with the prevention of poor health before it actually occurs by emphasizing a healthy lifestyle.

3. The role of _____ _____ includes the right to be excused from social responsibility and other normal social roles.

4. The process of giving all aspects of health and illness an exclusively medical meaning is referred to as the _____ _____ _____.

5. _____ _____ is an aspect of health care that is concerned with the diagnosis, advice, and treatment of illnesses by certified medical professionals such as doctors and nurses.

6. While advanced medical technology has enabled doctors to use _____ measures to keep patients with severe illnesses alive, it has also contributed to the high cost of medical care in the United States.

7. Withdrawing the vital life support system from a terminally ill person is referred to as _____ _____, whereas actively killing a severely ill person who would otherwise live, as an act of mercy, is _____ _____.

8. Many industrial nations--such as Britain, Norway, and Sweden--provide universal medical care to all of their citizenry through a _____ _____ _____.

9. The United States, with its strong valuation on private enterprise, provides medical care on a _____ basis--where the individual patient is responsible for paying the fees charged.

10. An adequate _____ _____ system includes the provision of medical care, policies that minimize the chances of accidents, a clean environment, and ecological protection.

PART V

SOCIAL CHANGE AND THE MODERN WORLD

CHAPTER 19

THE MASS MEDIA IN CONTEMPORARY SOCIETY

I.   LEARNING OBJECTIVES

1.   To understand the importance of mass media in modern society.
2.   To become familiar with the sociological theories and concepts that attempt to explain the impact of mass media on society.
3.   To understand how news is created, including what sociologists refer to as "agenda-setting," determining what counts as news and what does not, and "framing," the way in which news shapes audience perceptions.
4.   To become familiar with the ways in which news reflects and reinforces gender, racial, and ethnic stereotypes and inequalities.
5.   To understand the extent and impact of media violence.
6.   To become familiar with the globalization of mass media, including the spread of images of American life and democratic ideas throughout the world.

II.   CHAPTER OVERVIEW

The purpose of this chapter is to introduce you to the mass media in contemporary society, especially how it influences daily life and contributes to the globalization of politics and culture.

A.   **Introduction: Hooked on Television.** This section opens with a discussion of the media coverage of the 1991 Persian Gulf war and the role of the news media in relaying information about Middle Eastern politics and the events leading up to the war.

   1.   Define *mass media*.

   2.   What were the findings of the survey conducted by Center for Studies in Communication regarding the media as "information providers"?

   3.   What percentage of American households have at least one television set? How many hours per week do American children under the age of eleven watch TV?

B.   **The Importance of Mass Media in Modern Society**

   1.   Define *mass-mediated culture*.

      a.   How did the invention of the printing press in the 15th century change human communication?

      b.   Define *mass audience*.

      c.   What is the importance of "one-directional" flow of information? Give an example illustrating how one-direction flow of information has been used to influence public perception.

C.   **The Impact of Mass Media.**   In this section you are introduced to the sociological theories of mass media in modern society.

   1.   What is the primary assumption of the *limited effects* theory of mass media?

      a.   What prompted the emergence of limited effects theory?

      b.   Define *mass society*.

      c.   Briefly characterize the findings of the small-group studies on the impact of media on shaping public perception.

      d.   What are two fundamental critiques of limited effects theory?

         (1)

(2)

2. What is the main argument of *class dominant* theory?

   a. What evidence do class-dominant theorists rely on to support their view of the media?

   b. According to class-dominant theory, why are the news media--newspapers, radio, and television--unable to be impartial in reporting the news?

   c. Why are class-dominant theorists concerned about the sale of advertising as a source of revenue for most forms of mass media?

   d. According to class-dominant theory, how does modern technology encourage concentration of power?

   e. What are two critiques of class-dominant theory?

3. What is the primary concern of *culturalist theory*?

   a. Identify the two streams of culturalist research.

      (1)

      (2)

   b. What is the primary concern of *audience relations* research?

c. List some of the ways in which viewers actively participate in the audience-media relationship.

d. What has audience relations research revealed about the relationship between college students' race and their interpretations of music videos?

e. What are two fundamental critiques of culturalist theory of the media?

D. **Producing the News: How "News" is Created**

1. Your text points out that the news is not simply reported; rather, it is defined, selected, and constructed by those who work in the news industry. Sociologists refer to this process of news production as *agenda-setting*. What is *agenda-setting* and what are the two areas of sociological concern?

2. Define the term *framing*.

   a. List the three ways in which news organizations frame audience perceptions.

      (1)

      (2)

      (3)

3. What are the *official sources* of information?

   a. Briefly explain why journalists privilege official sources of information?

4.   What is the *categorization of news*? List some of the news categories used by media, and explain how such categorizations define what is newsworthy.

    a.   How does the categorization of news determine how coverage is framed and distributed throughout the pages of a paper or in the lineup of television news stories?

    b.   What is the effect of the categorization of news on the representation of women in news reports?

5.   What reasons are given for the *over-simplification of complex issues*?

    a.   What effect does the over-simplification of complex news issues have on the presentation of the news?

    b.   List and briefly describe three ways in which simplification achieved?

        (1)

        (2)

        (3)

E.   **Stereotyping and Inequality in News and Entertainment.** The purpose of this section is to help you become familiar with the ways in which news media reflect and reinforce social inequality and gender, race, and ethnic stereotypes.

    1.   Briefly characterize the racial and ethnic composition of the media profession.

    2.   Describe the problem-oriented news coverage of racial and ethnic minorities.

a. How does problem-oriented coverage foster a "blame the victim" attitude?

3. Briefly describe how Blacks, Hispanics, Asians, and American Indians are depicted in the entertainment media.

 a. After several years of fighting negative stereotyping, what is the current status of Blacks, Latinos, and other racial groups in the entertainment media?

 b. Rap music began as black dance music during the 1970s and is one of the most enduring forms of music to emerge in the past two decades. Briefly describe the focus of the lyrics to most rap music. What argument do rap musicians make in support of their lyrics?

4. Briefly characterize the status of women in the media profession. How is women's under-representation in the media profession explained?

 a. How are women portrayed in the entertainment media?

F. **Violence and the Media**

1. While studies have linked television violence to aggression in children, little effort has been made by networks to reduce violent programming. How many violent acts are there per hour during prime time viewing? During the Saturday morning children's shows?

 a. How many murders and other violent acts has the average junior high school child viewed?

b. Three major reports on the relationship between media violence and aggression were conducted over the past 20 years. List who conducted the three studies and state what they concluded about the relationship between media violence and aggression.

(1)

(2)

(3)

Conclusion: _____
_____
_____

c. What are some of the other conclusions scholars have drawn concerning the effects of viewing media violence?

d. What have studies of media violence against women concluded about the effects of exposure of undergraduate males to sexually violent materials?

G. **Talk Radio and American Politics.** Talk radio has become an important social and political medium. In this section you are introduced to the rise of talk radio and its role in society.

1. Briefly describe the role of talk radio and radio personalities in American politics.

2. Describe the social, economic, and political composition of today's talk radio audience.

a. Talk show host, Jim Hightower, described talk radio as "a megaphone for anger." Please explain.

H. **Mass Media and the New Information Technologies.** Mass media includes forms of communication that permit a one-way flow of information. In this section you are introduced to new information technologies that permit a two-way flow of information via telephone lines, cable, or satellite.

1.   According to a recent national survey, audiences are increasingly critical of the mass media. What percentage of adults surveyed report having less confidence in the news? What percentage felt that media have too much influence?

2.   How does a two-way flow of information challenge the power and influence held by one-way mass media?

3.   Why are sociologists skeptical about predictions that new two-way information technologies may give rise to new democratic forms of governance?

4.   Define technological literacy, and explain how stratification favors those who are technologically literate.

5.   Critical Thinking Box 19.2 raises the question of whether new technologies will serve to "strengthen the hand of 'big brother'. What argument does Herb Brody make concerning the new technology?

I.   **Globalization and the Media: "It all came from there."** In this section you are introduced to the way in which the mass media contribute to the globalization of culture throughout the world.

1.   The vast majority of one-way information flow is generated from industrial nations, particularly from the United States to the rest of the world. Why is this imbalance in global information flow a concern for some countries?

2.   What argument is made by the field of *development communication* concerning the media's democratizing influence?

a.   Give an example illustrating how the media promote democratic ideals.

III.   STUDENT ACTIVITIES

1.   The mass media often reinforces gender, racial, and ethnic stereotypes. How are these groups represented in the television programs that you watch? Do you think that women are under represented as sources and topics of news stories in the newspapers you read or the television and radio programs you listen to? Do news accounts of women appear on the front pages of your newspaper? If so, do the news accounts mention their gender, physical appearance, clothing, and marital status? How many news stories in your local paper are written by women? By men? Do news accounts of racial and ethnic minorities focus on social problems? In your opinion, do the television programs you watch present all minorities as having joined the American upper-middle class?

2.   Which theory of media influence appeals to you--limited effects theory, class-dominant theory, or culturalist theory? Do you think that the media has minimal impact on people's attitudes and perceptions? Do you think that the attitudes and perceptions of the mass audience of newspapers, television, and radio are controlled by powerful media conglomerates? Or, do you think that people are active participants in interpreting the news?

IV.   KEY TERMS

Listed below are some of the key terms that are introduced in Chapter 19. After you have read the chapter in your text and worked through the overview on the preceding pages, test your recall by writing the definitions of the terms in the space provided. You may check your work by referring to the *Key Terms* section at the end of the chapter in your text.

agenda-setting _____

_____

audience relations_____

_____

categorization of the news _____

_____

framing _____

_____

mass audience_____

_____

mass media _____

_____

mass society _____

_____

official sources _____

_____

personalizing the news _____

_____

technological literacy _____

_____

V.   TEST QUESTIONS

Multiple-Choice Questions
Choose the correct answer from the choices provided.

1.   The mass media:
     a.   is characterized primarily by a one-way flow of information.
     b.   is impartial in presenting the news.
     c.   represents women and men equally as sources and topics of the news.
     d.   functions primarily to mirror society.

2.   Limited effects theory argues that:
     a.   people play an active role in creating meaning out of what they receive from the media.
     b.   society is dominated by a relatively small, powerful elite whose viewpoint the media reflects.
     c.   the media has little impact on people's attitudes and perceptions, since audiences are selective.
     d.   people are mindless consumers of information, never questioning what they read in the newspaper or see on television.

3.   Culturalist theory of media influence is criticized for:
     a.   conducting research that is ahistorical.
     b.   ignoring the economics of media production.
     c.   focusing on white middle class audiences, while ignoring other groups.
     d.   all of the above.

4.   Agenda-setting refers to:
     a.   the way in which television viewers select and interpret the news.
     b.   the way the news media determines what counts as news and what does not.
     c.   the ways in which the content of the news shapes viewers perceptions.
     d.   the strategies that media conglomerates use in shaping news coverage.

5. Class-dominant theory of media influence argues that:
    a. newspapers, radios, and television are dominated by commercial concerns.
    b. people engaged in the day-to-day operations of the media independently influence how news is covered and presented.
    c. people are discriminating consumers of the media information and images they receive.
    d. none of the above.

6. Audience relations research is concerned with:
    a. the relationship between different groups of television viewing audiences.
    b. the ways in which the media provide a set of meanings that viewers interpret according to their own cultural understandings.
    c. how the news media reinforce gender, racial, and ethnic stereotypes.
    d. the extent to which television news programs are watched by different racial and ethnic groups.

7. Which is not a framing device used by the news media?
    a. official sources
    b. over-simplification of complex issues
    c. categorization of the news
    d. development communication

8. As defined by your text, mass society is one whose members:
    a. lack social ties.
    b. are isolated.
    c. are easily manipulated by the media.
    d. all of the above.

9. Which is not true of official sources of the news?
    a. They claim to speak on behalf of larger constituencies.
    b. They hold greater weight and credibility.
    c. They have limited influence on reporters' perspectives and opinions.
    d. They are well-positioned to control the flow and content of the news.

10. The field of development communication is concerned with:
    a. how communications media develop in particular countries or regions.
    b. how the dissemination of media contributes to the movement from coercive forms of government to more democratic forms.
    c. the origin and development of mass media.
    d. none of the above.

261

True/False Questions
For each of the following statements, decide whether the statement is true or false. Write your answer in the space provided.

_____ 1. American children under the age of eleven average 28 hours a week watching television.

_____ 2. One of the most important features of mass media is its two-directional flow.

_____ 3. Limited effects theory arose during the 1940s and 1950s in response to a fear that in modern society the media would become an all-powerful tool of business and government.

_____ 4. The news media is completely neutral in its choice and presentation of the news.

_____ 5. Class-dominant theorists argue that because the media are dominated by commercial concerns they are unable to be impartial in their coverage and presentation of the news.

_____ 6. Audience relations research is primarily concerned with the way in which relations are formed between groups of television viewers.

_____ 7. Culturalist theory argues that viewers are active participants in their choice and interpretation of the news.

_____ 8. Personalizing the news refers to the way in which individuals interpret the news to fit their own life experiences.

_____ 9. Women and men are equally represented in the media profession and as sources and topics of news stories.

_____ 10. News accounts of racial and ethnic minorities often focus on problems, fostering a "blame the victim" attitude.

Matching Exercise
For each of the following terms, identify the correct definition and write the appropriate letter in the space provided.

a. audience relations
b. categorization of news
c. culturalist theory of media influence
d. development communication
e. limited effects theory of media influence
f. class-dominant theory of media influence

g. mass audience
h. mass society
i. mass-mediated culture
j. personalizing the news

_____ 1. is one in which the mass media plays a key role in shaping and creating our cultural perceptions.

_____ 2. a large collection of people who receive messages that are not directed at them as individuals, but rather as a group.

_____ 3. argues that the media has minimal impact on peoples attitudes and perceptions.

_____ 4. one whose members are rootless, isolated, lacking in strong social ties, and thus defenseless against various forms of manipulation.

_____ 5. argues that the media are increasingly controlled by a handful of large, powerful media conglomerates, resulting in a sharp decline in competition.

_____ 6. a field of research concerned with the ways in which the media provide a set of meanings that are interpreted by views according to their own cultural understandings.

_____ 7. acknowledges that the media is controlled by a small number of conglomerates, but emphasizes the role of audiences and media workers in actively shaping the audience-media relationship.

_____ 8. determining whether or not a given event "fits" into some pre-existing category or "beat."

_____ 9. presenting the news as resulting exclusively from the efforts of individuals rather than underlying social forces.

_____ 10. argues that the widespread dissemination of newspapers, radio, and eventually television is central to a society's movement from coercive forms of government to truly democratic forms.

Completion
Write in the word(s) that best completes each of the following statements. To check your work, refer to the answer key at the end of this study guide.

1. _____ theory of media argues that society is dominated by a relatively small, powerful elite, whose viewpoint the media overwhelmingly tends to reflect.

2.   Forms of communication that permit a one-way flow of information from a single source to a large audience are called _____ _____.

3.   According to _____ _____ theory of media, the media has minimal impact on people's attitudes and perceptions, since audiences are selective in what they watch, perceive, and recall.

4.   A _____ culture is one in which the mass media plays a key role in shaping and creating cultural perceptions.

5.   The _____ theory of media argues that people play an active role in creating their own cultural meanings out of what they receive from the media.

6.   _____ _____ is a field of communication research that argues that the widespread dissemination of newspapers, radio, and television is central to a society's movement toward democratic forms of government.

7.   A framing device that consists of representing the news as resulting from the efforts of individuals rather than underlying social forces is referred to as _____ the news.

8.   Some sociologists argue that new communications technologies may result in stratification of society based on _____ _____, mastery of the most recent technical innovations.

9.   Determining what counts as news and what does not is referred to as _____.

10.   Much of what is called "news" is obtained from _____ _____, government authorities, designated spokesperson, and others who have some specialized expertise on a topic and who speak on behalf of larger constituencies.

CHAPTER 20

POPULATION, URBANIZATION, AND THE ENVIRONMENT

I. LEARNING OBJECTIVES

1. To become familiar with the relationship between population growth, industrialization, urbanization, and the environment.
2. To become familiar with demography and with the concepts and theories that organize demographic analysis.
3. To understand the process of urbanization and its impact on modern life.
4. To understand how population growth, industrialization, and urbanization contribute to global environmental problems, and to become familiar with efforts to deal with those problems.

II. CHAPTER OVERVIEW

The purpose of this chapter is to introduce you to the relationship between population growth, urbanization, and the environment.

A. **Introduction: A Global Problem.** This section opens with David Suzuki's comments on the environmental problems facing our world today, and their likely effect on our world during the next century.

    1.   David Suzuki draws our attention to the environmental devastation of the tropical rainforests. Briefly describe the Amazon region, including its size, plant and animal life, and its potential for science.

        a.   What economic, political, and social factors contribute to the destruction of the rainforests in Brazil and other tropical countries?

B. **Global Population Growth.** In this section you are introduced to the subfield of sociology known as demography and to many of the concepts and theories that organize demographic analyses.

    1.   Define the term *demography*.

a.   List the four factors that determine annual population growth and decline.

(1)

(2)

(3)

(4)

b.   What is a *population pyramid?*

c.   What is the general fertility/mortality profile of low-income preindustrial countries?   List two or three countries that fit this profile.   Draw or describe the population pyramid of these countries.

d.   What is the general fertility/mortality profile of high-income industrial nations? List two or three countries that fit this profile. Draw or describe the population pyramid of these countries.

e.   Demographers estimate fertility and population growth on the basis of *crude birth rates* and *age-specific fertility rates.* Define these terms, and specify which is a more accurate measure.

f.   Define the term *cohort,* and briefly explain how cohort analyses of fertility can be projected into the future.

g.   Demographers estimate mortality on the basis of *crude death rates, age-specific mortality rates.* Define these terms, and specify which is a more accurate measure.

h.   Mortality is also estimated on the basis of *life expectancy.* Define this term, and specify the general life expectancy pattern for males and females in the United States.

      (1)   Compare the average life expectancies for males and females in the United States, Hong Kong, and the African country of Sierra Leone.

    i.   List some of the factors that make it difficult to make predictions about population growth.

    j.   Briefly explain why the number of young girls who constitute potential mothers at some time in the future is so important in population forecasting. Give an example illustrating this point.

2.   What is the main assumption of the *theory of the demographic transition*?

    a.   According to this view, what are the three stages of population change that most societies seem to go through?

        (1)

        (2)

        (3)

    b.   Why were strong beliefs and institutions governing fertility developed in agriculturally-based preindustrial societies?

    c.   What effect did industrialization have on fertility and mortality?

3.   What is the fundamental critique of the theory of the demographic transition?

4.   Why are programs to control population growth in low-income countries so controversial?

5.   Your text points out that the first 'doubling' of the human population took sixteen centuries to occur, and the second 'doubling' took only two. How many years is the third doubling of the population expected to take?

        a.   What was the global population in 1993?

        b.   What is the projected population for the year 2030?

        c.   What percent of the population in 2030 is expected to live in low-income nations?

6.   British social philosopher Thomas Malthus observed that the *population grows exponentially*. Briefly explain Malthus's theory.

        a.   Define the *doubling time* exhibited by exponential population increases.

        b.   According to Malthus, what is the relationship between exponential population growth and the world's food supply? What outcome did Malthus predict unless humans take steps to control population growth?

        c.   What is the primary critique of Malthus's theory?

        d.   Define the term *doubling fallacy*.

7.   What was Karl Marx's main critique of Malthus's theory of overpopulation?

        a.   What did Marx identify as the source of human suffering?

b.   According to Marx, what is the cause of the apparent scarcity of resources?

c.   How has Marx's criticism of Malthus held up over time?

d.   What is the primary critique of Marx's theory?

C.   **Urbanization.** This section provides an introduction to many of the concepts used in the sociological study of urbanization, and to the history and development of modern urban forms.

1.   Give the sociological definitions of the following terms:

Rural: _____

Urban: _____

City: _____

Metropolis: _____

Metropolitan
Statistical Area (MSA): _____

Consolidated Metropolitan
Statistical Area (CMSA): _____

2.   According to the 1990 census, there were 284 MSAs and CMSAs in the United States. What proportion of the American population lives in MSAs and CMSAs?

a.   List the five largest CMSAs in the United States.

(1)

(2)

(3)

(4)

269

(5)

3. Describe *preindustrial cities*, and state when they first appeared.

    a. How did the production of *agricultural surplus* contribute to the emergence of preindustrial cities?

    b. Who resided in preindustrial cities?

4. Briefly explain how industrialization contributed to urbanization in *industrial cities*.

    a. Describe the living conditions in *industrial cities*.

    b. German sociologist Ferdinand Toennies contrasted traditional rural life, *Gemeinschaft*, with the new urban cities, *Gesellschaft*. Define these terms, and explain Toennies's view concerning the emergence of industrial cities.

    c. During the 1920s and 1930s, researchers at the University of Chicago became interested in the study of city life. What was the primary focus of these studies? What did these studies conclude concerning the relationship between urbanization and social life?

5. What is *human ecology*?

    a. According to human ecologists, what determines the physical organization of cities?

b. Describe the Burgess "concentric zone" model of the city.

c. What is the primary critique of the ecological approach to the study of urbanization and city life?

6. What are the principle forces shaping cities in the United States?

a. What is the *urban growth machine* as termed by sociologists John Logan and Harvey Molotch? According to Logan and Molotch, who makes up the urban growth machine?

b. Briefly describe how the urban growth machine operated in the post-World War II development of cities in the United States, listing some of the programs that contributed to urbanization.

c. How has modern technology contributed to the expansion of urban boundaries?

d. What problems arise for cities, especially inner cities, as postindustrial society moves beyond the urban fringe? What percent of America's poor lived in central cites in 1987?

e. Define *suburb*, and explain why suburbs are growing so rapidly in the United States.

7. Poverty, segregation, and discrimination are common in American cities.

a. According to the 1990 census, what percent of all African Americans live in neighborhoods that are almost entirely black?

b. What percent of the American population would have to move to achieve fully integrated neighborhoods?

c. Segregation is due, in part, to the preferences people have about where they live. But it is also a result of discrimination. Define the following terms, and explain how each contribute to segregation.

(1) *Redlining*

(2) *Urban renewal*

(3) *Gentrification*

8. The problems of urbanization are being experienced by many countries in the world. Using Map 20.1 in your text, list the world's 10 largest metropolitan areas in 1991.

a. What percent of the world's population is expected to live in urban areas by the year 2000?

b. What are some of the problems that arise with rapid urbanization, especially for low-income countries?

9. What are *global cities?* Give two or three examples of global cities.

a. What role has the new information technologies had in the emergence of global cities?

10. Saskia Sassen has identified four principal functions of global cities. List the four functions below.

a.

b.

c.

d.

D.   **Population Growth, Urbanization, and the Environment.** In this section you are introduced to the impact of increased population growth and rapid urbanization on global resources and environment.

1.   Which three countries make up 42 percent of the world's population?

a.   What concern arises with the industrialization of these countries?

b.   Your textbook mentions that many low-income nations owe enormous debt to more wealthy nations. Explain how this contributes to problems in the development of low-income nations.

2.   Urbanization and industrialization create many environmental problems. Briefly explain the impact urbanization and industrialization can have on a city's supply of food, water, and fuel.

3.   Silenced Voices Box 20.2 discusses the impact of environmental problems on low-income and minority people. Briefly describe how global environmental problems are experienced locally by these groups of people.

4.   What is the *greenhouse effect*, and how has the global loss of forests and energy waste contributed to it?

a.   Define *global warming*.

b. What is the *ozone layer*, and what is causing its depletion?

c. Why are low-income nations expected to become a major source of greenhouse gases as they industrialize?

d. Briefly describe Donella and Dennis Meadows' 1972 study, <u>The Limits to Growth</u>. What is the researchers' main argument concerning planetary economy and ecology?

e. Define *sustainable development*, and explain how it might help to preserve our global environment.

E. **Globalization: Progress Toward Sustainable Development**. In this chapter you have been introduced to the problems that arise in the interaction between population, urbanization, and industrialization. In this section you will learn about the steps that have been taken to find solutions to those problems.

1. Briefly explain how global institutions are important in dealing with the environmental problems facing our world.

2. There has been some progress toward controlling global population growth. Why, then, is there resistance in the United States government and in low-income nations to population control efforts?

a. Why is the changing role of women in the global economy thought to be important in global population control?

3. What steps have been made to protect the ozone layer by limiting the use of chlorofluorocarbons (CFCs)?

4. What was the purpose of the June 1992 United Nations Conference on the Environment and Development in Rio de Janeiro?

    a. What did high-income nations seek to achieve from the Conference?

    b. What did low-income nations seek to achieve from the Conference?

III. STUDENT ACTIVITIES

1. This chapter has introduced you to the problems of poverty, segregation, and discrimination in American cities. As defined in this chapter, do you live in a city, the suburb of a city, or a rural area? Is your community racially and ethnically integrated? Or, is it segregated by race and ethnicity? Do you believe that redlining or blockbusting are a problem in your community? Is your community undergoing gentrification? If so, has it had a favorable or an adverse effect on any group of people?

2. German sociologist Ferdinand Tonnies drew a comparison between traditional life and urban life of the early industrial cities, with the former (*Gemeinschaft*) based on intimate relationships and the latter on impersonal relationships (*Gesellschaft*). Do you think that Toennies' characterization holds true for urban life today? Are relationships in modern urban life impersonal? Have traditional beliefs and values given way to cold calculation and impersonal reason? What evidence of traditional life still exists in modern society? Do you agree with Georg Simmel, a contemporary of Toennies, that the impersonality of urban life creates new opportunities for freedom and creativity?

IV.   KEY TERMS

Listed below are some of the key terms that are introduced in Chapter 20. After you have read the chapter in your text and worked through the overview on the preceding pages, test your recall by writing the definitions of the terms in the space provided. You may check your work by referring to the *Key Terms* section at the end of the chapter in your text.

age-specific fertility rates _____

_____

age-specific mortality rates_____

_____

cohort_____

_____

demography _____

_____

gentrification _____

_____

global cities _____

_____

industrial cities _____

_____

net migration _____

_____

redlining _____

_____

urbanization _____

_____

V.   TEST QUESTIONS

Multiple-Choice Questions
Choose the correct answer from the choices provided.

1.   Annual population growth or decline in a country is a result of the number of people who:
   a.   are born during the year.
   b.   die during the year.
   c.   move into and out of a country during the year.
   d.   all of the above

2. Predicting future population growth is difficult because of:
    a. family planning programs.
    b. epidemics (such as AIDS).
    c. the development of new drugs.
    d. all of the above

3. The theory of demographic transition argues that industrialization will lead to:
    a. an increase in mortality
    b. a decline in fertility.
    c. an increase in mortality and fertility.
    d. a decrease in mortality and an increase in fertility.

4. By the year 2030, the global population is expected to reach:
    a. 11 billion.
    b. 15 billion.
    c. 22 billion.
    d. 50 billion.

5. The idea that population grows exponentially originated with the work of:
    a. Karl Marx.
    b. Emile Durkheim.
    c. Thomas Malthus.
    d. Ferdinand Toennies.

6. The *doubling fallacy* refers to the false assumption that:
    a. a rate of population increase can be sustained indefinitely.
    b. families will limit their offspring to two children.
    c. population and food supply grow and decline at the same rate.
    d. none of the above.

7. As defined in your text, a permanent settlement of people who depend on others for the production of food is:
    a. a rural area.
    b. a city.
    c. a metropolis.
    d. urban.

8. The use of the terms *Gemeinschaft* (community) and *Gesellschaft* (society) to characterize traditional life and urban life, respectively, is most clearly associated with the work of:
    a. Ferdinand Toennies.
    b. Emile Durkheim.
    c. Georg Simmel.
    d. Thomas Malthus.

9.   The study of human ecology is concerned with:
      a.   global environmental problems (e.g., global warming).
      b.   the spatial organization of people in urban environments.
      c.   ecological urban renewal of inner cities.
      d.   the way in which people interact with one another in urban environments.

10.   Which of the following is <u>not</u> considered to be a part of the urban growth machine:
      a.   newspapers.
      b.   lawyers.
      c.   land developers.
      d.   individual home owners.

True/False Questions
For each of the following statements, decide whether the statement is true or false. Write your answer in the space provided.

_____   1.   Crude birth and death rates are less accurate than age-specific birth and death rates.

_____   2.   Life expectancy is a measure of overall mortality of a society.

_____   3.   In the United States, the life expectancy at birth is longer for males than for females.

_____   4.   High fertility societies typically have small numbers of children.

_____   5.   Thomas Malthus claimed that while population grows exponentially, food supply grows at a constant rate.

_____   6.   Karl Marx argued that the inequitable distribution of resources, rather than overpopulation, was a central concern facing modern society.

_____   7.   The quarter of the world's population that lives in high-income industrialized nations currently consumes three-quarters of the world's resources.

_____   8.   Redlining is a policy that banks and other lending institutions use to bring about racial and ethnic integration of neighborhoods.

_____   9.   The release of carbon dioxide and other industrial gases into the atmosphere contributes to a _greenhouse effect_, where heat is trapped at the planet's surface.

_____   10.   Sustainable development calls for an end to all economic development programs to preserve the world's environment.

Matching Exercise

For each of the following terms, identify the correct definition and write the appropriate letter in the space provided.

a.   city
b.   demographic transition
c.   doubling fallacy
d.   doubling time
e.   exponential population growth
f.   fertility
g.   gentrification
h.   greenhouse effect
i.   mortality
j.   population pyramid

_____   1.   deaths in a population.

_____   2.   a process by which upper-income professionals buy low-cost downtown housing, fix it up, move in, and thereby convert neighborhoods from low- to high-income, displacing the poor as a result.

_____   3.   reproductive performance, as indicated by the number of live births actually born to a woman.

_____   4.   a theory that argues that industrialization is associated with movement from high fertility and mortality to low fertility and mortality.

_____   5.   a constant rate of population growth, resulting in a population that increases by an increasing amount with each passing year.

_____   6.   a graph that represents the composition of a country's population by age and sex.

_____   7.   a layer of gases in the upper atmosphere that traps heat at the planet's surface.

_____   8.   the false assumption that a given rate of population increase can be sustained indefinitely.

_____   9.   a permanent settlement of people who depend on others for the production of food.

_____   10. under exponential growth, the number of years it takes for the total population to double.

Completion

Write in the word(s) that best completes each of the following statements. To check your work, refer to the answer key at the end of this study guide.

1. Cities emerged when advanced agricultural techniques permitted societies to produce more food than they needed for immediate survival, resulting in an _____ _____.

2. The _____ _____ _____ is the number of births each year per 1,000 people; whereas the _____ _____ _____ is the number of deaths each year per 1,000 people.

3. Ferdinand Toennies drew a distinction between traditional life, which he termed _____, and urban life, termed _____.

4. In almost all societies, the _____ _____ at birth is longer for females than for males.

5. Many who are concerned about global environmental problems have called for _____ _____, programs that would create economic growth while preserving the environment.

6. _____ _____ is a subfield of sociology, developed at the University of Chicago, concerned with the study of spatial organization of people in their urban environment.

7. _____ _____ refers to a federal government program that provides funds to localities for fixing up blighted areas.

8. _____ _____ is a projected increase in the average planetary temperatures by 3-8 degrees Fahrenheit by the middle of the next century, resulting from the *greenhouse effect*.

9. In the United States, _____ refers to any human settlement of fewer than 2,500 people; while _____ is used to describe a concentration of people engaged in non-agricultural activities.

10. According to John Logan and Harvey Molotch, a principal force in shaping cities is the _____ _____ _____, persons and institutions that have a stake in growth in the value of urban land.

CHAPTER 21

SOCIAL CHANGE, COLLECTIVE BEHAVIOR, AND SOCIAL MOVEMENTS

I.   LEARNING OBJECTIVES

1.   To become familiar with the sociological theories of societal change.
2.   To understand the relationship between collective behavior and social movements.
3.   To become familiar with the theories and various forms of collective behavior.
4.   To become familiar with the principal types of social movements, why they arise, and their role in shaping history.
5.   To understand how globalization has created new opportunities for the formation of "new" social movements.

II.   CHAPTER OVERVIEW

The purpose of this chapter is to introduce you to the way in which sociologists have approached the study of social change.

A.   **Introduction: Approaches to Understanding Social Change**

   1.   There are a number of ways in which sociologists have approached the study of social change.   List and identify the focus of the three approaches that are mentioned in the introduction to this chapter.

      a.

      b.

      c.

B.   **Theories of Societal Change.**   In this section you are introduced to some of the terms and concepts that organization sociological thinking about social change, and to three theoretical approaches to the study of social change.

   1.   List the three theoretical perspectives on societal change.

      a.

      b.

      c.

2.   What is the primary assumption of functionalist theories of social change, and with whom is the origin of this approach to social change most closely associated?

      a.   Briefly describe Herbert Spencer's view of social change.

      b.   According to Spencer, what distinguishes premodern from modern societies?

      c.   Name the two functionalist theorists who shared Spencer's beliefs about social change.

      d.   Early functionalist theories were *evolutionary theories*. What is the primary assumption of evolutionary theories? Then, list and define the two forms of evolutionary theory.

           (1)

           (2)

      e.   Briefly explain what Emile Durkheim and, more recently, Talcott Parsons believed about societies reaching an *equilibrium state*.

      f.   What is the primary critique of evolutionary theories of societal change?

3.   What is the underlying assumption of *conflict theories of societal change*?

      a.   Evolutionary theorists attribute social change to external forces. To what do conflict theorists attribute social change? Give an example of how social transformation occurs.

      b.   What is the primary critique of conflict theories of societal change?

4.   What is the primary assumption of *rise and falls theories* of social change?

      a.   Give an example of how rise and fall theories are common in many religious myths.

      b.   How are rise and fall theories of social change evidenced in Paul Kennedy's study of national power and decline, *The Rise and Fall of Great Powers*?

      c.   Max Weber is one of the most important theorists to study social change as a cyclical process. Briefly describe Weber's views in this regard.

      d.   What is the primary critique of cyclical or rise and fall theories of societal change?

C.   **Sources of Social Change: Collective Behavior.** In this section you are introduced to the theories of collective behavior.

1.   Define *collective behavior*.

      a.   Under what conditions does collective behavior occur?

      b.   Who is Gustave LeBon?

c.   Define the term *crowd*, and list some of the characteristics of crowd behavior.

2.   Briefly describe the origins of the contemporary study of collective behavior, including where it originated and with which researchers.

a.   What are the three principal approaches to the study of collective behavior?

(1)

(2)

(3)

3.   What is the primary assumption of *contagion theories* of collective behavior?

a.   What are the names of the researchers with whom this approach originated?

b.   Briefly explain what Herbert Blumer means by "raw imitation."

c.   What sorts of studies of collective behavior have been conducted by contagion theorists?

d.   What is the primary critique of contagion theories of collective behavior?

4.   What is the primary assumption underlying *emergent norm theories* of collective behavior?

a.   Briefly describe Turner and Killian's theory of collective behavior.

b.   What are two critiques of emergent norm theories of collective behavior?

5.   What is the primary assumption of *value-added theory* of collective behavior, and what is the name of the researcher with whom this theory is associated?

a.   List and give a description of the micro- and macro-level factors that must converge for collective behavior to occur.

        Factors   Description

        (1)

        (2)

        (3)

        (4)

        (5)

        (6)

b.   Smelser's theory has been criticized for overemphasizing the reactive elements of collective behavior. Please explain.

6.   Your text mentions several types of collective behavior. Use the chart below to define and give an example of each type. In the last column, describe the conditions that give rise to each form of collective behavior.

        Definition   Example   Conditions

Riots

Fads

Fashions

Panics

Crazes

Rumors

a.   Briefly explain Georg Simmel's view of the sociological implications of *fashions*.

b.   Describe the study of rumors conducted by Allport and Postman. What did this study reveal about *rumors*?

D.   **Social Movements**

1.   How are theories of social movements distinguished from theories of collective behavior?

a.   Define and briefly characterize *social movements*.

b.   Who are social movements typically comprised of?

c.   On what basis are social movements classified?

d.   List below the five different kinds of social movement, their principal aims, and give an example of each.

Social movement	Principal aims	Example

(1)

(2)

(3)

(4)

(5)

2. What is the primary distinction between reformist and revolutionary social movements?

3. How is it that the definition of a social movement as reactionary or revolutionary can depend on one's standpoint?

    a. Why are reactionary social movements expected to increase with globalization?

4. How have democratic forms of governance fueled the growth of social movements?

    a. A number of theories have been advanced in an effort to explain why people join together to bring about or resist social change. Briefly explain the focus of the following forms of analysis.

        Micro-level analysis: _____

        _____

        Organizational level analysis: _____

        _____

        Macro-level analysis: _____

        _____

5. What have micro-level studies revealed about what motivates individuals to become active members of social movements?

    a. Define the *free rider problem*, and explain how it effects social movements.

6.   Organizational-level studies focus on *social movement organizations (SMOs)*. Define and characterize SMOs.

       a.   What is the focus of *resource mobilization theory*?

       b.   How do resource mobilization theorists explain the emergence and success of social movements?

       c.   What part do governmental policies play in the success or failure of SMOs?

       d.   How can too much success undermine SMOs?

       e.   What is *goal displacement*? Give an example of the way in which goal displacement can effect an SMO.

7.   Social movements garner support from *grass roots organizing* and *conscience constiuents*. Define and give an example of each form of support.

8.   Macro-level studies focus on the societal conditions that give rise to social movements.

       a.   How do some economic and political systems encourage social movements? Give an example.

       b.   Briefly explain how prosperity can provide a basis for social movement activism.

c.   How can the spatial organization of a society impact social movements?

9.   Define *frame alignment*, and give an example of the way in which social movements achieve frame alignment with the larger society.

10.   What are *micro-mobilization contexts*?

a.   What sorts of incentives do micro-mobilization contexts offer people to get involved in social movement efforts?

E.   **Globalization and Social Change**

1.   Define and characterize *new social movements*.

a.   ACT-UP is a "new" social movement. According to sociologist John Gamson, what are the organization's two objectives, and what strategies are being used to achieve these objectives?

(1)

(2)

b.   New social movements tend to be single-issue oriented and highly fragmented. How do these factors contribute to or detract from the vitality and success of new social movements?

c.   Box 21.2 discusses the Mukti Sangharsh, a "new" social movement for environmental and women's rights in India. What are some of the characteristics of the Mukti Sangharsh that are common to other social movements, and how successful have they been in their efforts to bring about social change?

III. STUDENT ACTIVITIES

1. Micro-level theories of social movement attempt to explain why people join together to bring about social change. While early studies emphasized individual psychological factors that might account for social activism, more recent studies argue that participation is related to an identification with others who are similarly afflicted or to one's prior contact with movement members. Why do you think people join social movements? Do you think participation in a social movement is due to one's personality characteristics? Or, is participation a result of prior contact with movement members? If you have participated in a social movement, what motivated you to get involved? Is there a history of social activism in your family? Were you motivated to participate by a sense of moral rightness?

2. Your text presents three sociological theories of collective behavior, including: contagion theories, emergent norm theories, and value-added theory. Which of these theories do you think best explains collective behavior? Do you think that collective behavior is the result of raw imitation, as argued by contagion theories? Have you ever participated in collective behavior in which new norms emerge, as argued by emergent norm theories? Or, do you think that collective behavior is more the result of several converging factors, as argued by value-added theory?

IV. KEY TERMS

Listed below are some of the key terms that are introduced in Chapter 21. After you have read the chapter in your text and worked through the overview on the preceding pages, test your recall by writing the definitions of the terms in the space provided. You may check your work by referring to the *Key Terms* section at the end of the chapter in your text.

collective behavior _____

_____

craze _____

_____

crowds _____

_____

fad _____

_____

free rider problem _____

_____

micro-mobilization contexts _____

_____

rebellion _____

_____

riot _____

_____

social movement _____

_____

societal change _____

_____

V. TEST QUESTIONS

Multiple-Choice Questions
Choose the correct answer from the choices provided.

1. Which of the following is the principal aim of reformist social movements?
    a.   social change within existing economic and political systems
    b.   fundamental change in values, culture, and private life
    c.   fundamental change to existing social, political and economic system without defined vision
    d.   withdrawal from society to create a utopian community

2. Movements for homosexual rights, environmental issues, and India's Mukti Sangharsh are examples of:
    a.   communitarian social movements.
    b.   reactionary social movements.
    c.   "new" social movements.
    d.   reformist social movements.

3. Which of the following theoretical approaches attempt to explain participation in social movements in terms of individual personal gain or prior contact with movement members?
    a.   micro
    b.   macro
    c.   organizational
    d.   mobilization

4.   According to resource mobilization theory, successful social movements must have access to:
       a.   money.
       b.   means of communication.
       c.   dedicated, hard-working members.
       d.   all of the above

5.   Which of the following is <u>not</u> a factor contributing to the emergence, growth, and development of social movements?
       a.   the spatial organization of society
       b.   democratic forms of governance
       c.   a strong socialist party
       d.   the prosperity of a society

6.   Micro-mobilization contexts are:
       a.   small organizations that seek to achieve social change through concrete action
       b.   small group settings in which people are able to organize their beliefs and efforts around some social problem.
       c.   social movements that involve few resources and a relatively small number of people.
       d.   microcomputer systems that are set up to mobilize members of social movements who are geographically dispersed.

7.   Social movements that are concerned with the quality of private life, often advocating large-scale cultural changes in the way people think and act, are referred to as:
       a.   reactionary social movements.
       b.   rebellious social movements.
       c.   "new" social movements.
       d.   communitarian social movements.

8.   Which is <u>not</u> a form of collective behavior?
       a.   rumors
       b.   fads
       c.   panics
       d.   all of the above are forms of collective behavior

9.   Which of the following theories of societal change argues that all societies follow a single evolutionary path?
       a.   neoevolutionary theory
       b.   unilinear evolutionary theory
       c.   conflict theory
       d.   cyclical theory

10. The origin of the sociological study of collective behavior is most clearly linked to the writings of:
    a. Emile Durkheim.
    b. Max Weber.
    c. Gustave LeBon.
    d. Pitirim Sorokin.

True/False Questions

For each of the following statements, decide whether the statement is true or false. Write your answer in the space provided.

_____   1. Evolutionary theories regard all societies as moving in a single direction on some important dimension of societal change.

_____   2. Conflict theories depend on external forces, such as population growth or technological advances, to trigger societal change.

_____   3. Cyclical theories are common in the religious myths of many cultures, such as those that view social life as similar to the seasons of the year.

_____   4. As defined in your text, collective behavior is non-voluntary behavior.

_____   5. Collective behavior usually involves a disorganized aggregate of people.

_____   6. According to Herbert Blumer, collective behavior is a result of raw imitation whereby people stimulate and goad one another into movement.

_____   7. Both contagion and emergent-norm theories of collective behavior focus on micro-level factors.

_____   8. Crowds are less spontaneous than riots.

_____   9. Eating earthworms and goldfish, nude "streaking" in public, and wearing carefully worn-out Levis with torn knees are examples of fads.

_____   10. Rumor and panics may result from fears that stem from the loss of control over one's life in modern industrial society.

Matching Exercise

For each of the following terms, identify the correct definition and write the appropriate letter in the space provided.

a. communitarian social movement
b. conscience constituents
c. fashion
d. goal displacement
e. "new" social movement
f. panic
g. reactionary social movement
h. revolutionary social movement
i. rumor
j. unilinear evolutionary theories

_____ 1. movements that have arisen since the 1960s that are fundamentally concerned with the quality of private life, often advocating large-scale cultural changes in the ways that people think and act.

_____ 2. massive flight from something that is feared.

_____ 3. those theories that assume all societies follow a single evolutionary path.

_____ 4. unverified form of information that is transmitted informally.

_____ 5. a problem that occurs when a social movement organization's original goals become redirected toward enhancing the organization and its leadership.

_____ 6. a social movement that seeks to withdraw from the dominant society by creating its own ideal community.

_____ 7. a somewhat long-lasting style of imitative behavior or appearance.

_____ 8. a social movement that seeks to alter the existing social, political, and economic system in keeping with a vision of a new social order.

_____ 9. people who provide resources for a social movement organization who are not themselves members of the aggrieved group whom the organization champions.

_____ 10. a social movement that seeks to restore an earlier social system--often based on a mythical past--along with the traditional norms and values that once presumably accompanied it.

Completion

Write in the word(s) that best completes each of the following statements. To check your work, refer to the answer key at the end of this study guide.

1.	Herbert Spencer argued that what distinguished premodern from modern societies was _____, the development of increasing societal complexity through the creation of specialized social roles and institutions.

2.	Sociologists differ on whether _____ _____ takes place gradually or abruptly, and whether all societies change in the same direction.

3.	_____ _____ _____, such as the National Association for the Advancement of Colored People (NAACP), are formal organizations that seek to achieve social change through concrete action.

4.	_____ social movements attempt to bring about social change within the existing economic and political system.

5.	Many social movement organizations rely on _____ _____ _____ to mobilize support among ordinary members of the community.

6.	Some evolutionary theorists argue that societies eventually reach an _____ _____ in which no further change is likely to occur unless some external force sets changes in motion.

7.	_____ _____ is defined as voluntary, goal-oriented action that occurs in relatively disorganized situations, in which society's social norms and values cease to govern individual behavior.

8.	_____ _____ theorists argue that multiple paths to societal change exist, and are determined by the interplay between technology, environment, population, and social organization.

9.	_____ _____ _____ theories argue that societal change is one of growth and decline.

10.	According to _____ _____ theory, the rise and success of social movements is a result of differences in the availability of resources to different groups, and how effectively they utilize them.

ANSWER KEY

ANSWER KEY

CHAPTER 1 - The Sociological Perspective

Multiple-Choice
1. d	2. b	3. c	4. d	5. a
6. c	7. b	8. b	9. c	10. c

True/False
1. T	2. T	3. F	4. T	5. F
6. T	7. F	8. T	9. F	10. T

Matching
1. d	2. j	3. a	4. i	5. d
6. c	7. h	8. f	9. e	10. b

Completion
1. anomie
2. symbol
3. critical thinking
4. social facts
5. latent functions, manifest functions
6. diversity, inequality, globalization
7. race relations
8. ideal type
9. micro, macro
10. capitalists, proletariat

CHAPTER 2 - The Process of Inquiry

Multiple-Choice
1. d	2. a	3. b	4. d	5. d
6. c	7. a	8. c	9. c	10. d

True/False
1. T	2. F	3. F	4. T	5. F
6. T	7. T	8. F	9. T	10. F

Matching
1. d	2. a	3. j	4. e	5. g
6. i	7. c	8. h	9. f	10. b

Completion

1. dependent
3. nominal
5. spurious
7. replication
9. comparative-historical

2. concept
4. correlated
6. documentary analysis
8. research strategy
10. Hawthorn effect

CHAPTER 3 - Culture

Multiple-Choice

1. d	2. d	3. d	4. d	5. a
6. c	7. d	8. c	9. d	10. b

True/False

1. F	2. T	3. F	4. T	5. T
6. T	7. T	8. F	9. T	10. F

Matching

1. e	2. j	3. a	4. b	5. f
6. i	7. c	8. d	9. g	10. h

Completion

1. Culture, society
3. Social learning theorists
5. technology
7. Language
9. multicultural

2. popular culture
4. instincts
6. cultural lag
8. subculture
10. cultural diffusion

CHAPTER 4 - Societies

Multiple-Choice

1. d	2. d	3. a	4. b	5. d
6. b	7. d	8. a	9. d	10. a

True/False

1. T	2. F	3. T	4. T	5. F
6. T	7. F	8. T	9. T	10. F

Matching

1. i	2. c	3. d	4. g	5. e
6. h	7. a	8. j	9. b	10. f

Completion
1. social structure
2. social group
3. institutions
4. statuses
5. agriculture, industrial production
6. structural contradiction
7. surplus
8. stratified
9. productivity
10. socialism

CHAPTER 5 - *Socialization and Social Interaction*

Multiple-Choice
1. d	2. a	3. c	4. a	5. d
6. d	7. a	8. d	9. b	10. d

True/False
1. T	2. T	3. F	4. T	5. T
6. T	7. F	8. T	9. T	10. T

Matching
1. h	2. g	3. a	4. f	5. j
6. i	7. c	8. d	9. b	10. e

Completion
1. documentary method of interpretation
2. dramaturgical
3. Socialization
4. role-taking
5. super-ego
6. Agents of socialization
7. preconventional, conventional, postconventional
8. hidden curriculum
9. anticipatory socialization
10. Social learning

CHAPTER 6 - *Groups and Organizations*

Multiple-Choice
1. c	2. b	3. a	4. a	5. a
6. c	7. c	8. a	9. a	10. c

True/False
1. T	2. F	3. T	4. T	5. F
6. T	7. T	8. F	9. T	10. F

Matching
1. j	2. b	3. d	4. f	5. i
6. c	7. e	8. h	9. a	10. g

Completion
1. Formal organizations
2. primary, secondary
3. bureaucracy, democracy, oligarchy
4. transformational, transactional
5. Legitimate
6. network
7. increase, decreases, increases
8. triad
9. reference group
10. category

CHAPTER 7 - Deviance and Crime

Multiple-Choice

1. b	2. a	3. d	4. a	5. d
6. b	7. a	8. c	9. d	10. b

True/False

1. T	2. T	3. F	4. T	5. T
6. F	7. T	8. T	9. F	10. T

Matching

1. e	2. f	3. j	4. b	5. g
6. i	7. h	8. d	9. c	10. a

Completion
1. moral boundaries
2. goals, means
3. Structural contradiction
4. primary, secondary
5. differential association
6. criminologists
7. Uniform Crime Reports, National Crime Survey
8. Deterrence
9. pluralistic
10. property, victimless

CHAPTER 8 - Class and Stratification in the United States

Multiple-Choice

1. b	2. a	3. c	4. d	5. a
6. c	7. d	8. b	9. b	10. d

True/False

1. T	2. F	3. T	4. F	5. T
6. T	7. F	8. F	9. F	10. F

Matching

1. c	2. h	3. i	4. a	5. e
6. g	7. j	8. d	9. b	10. f

Completion
1. Wealth, income
2. Deinstitutionalization
3. Class dominance
4. cultural capital
5. inter-generational
6. upper
7. caste
8. Social stratification
9. contradictory class location
10. Social mobility

CHAPTER 9 - Global Inequality

Multiple-Choice

1. d	2. b	3. d	4. a	5. c
6. d	7. b	8. c	9. d	10. d

True/False

1. T	2. T	3. F	4. T	5. T
6. F	7. T	8. F	9. T	10. T

Matching

1. e	2. a	3. f	4. c	5. d
6. h	7. g	8. j	9. i	10. b

Completion
1. Market-oriented
2. Modernization
3. traditional
4. per-person gross national product
5. Dependency
6. colonialism
7. core, periphery, semiperiphery
8. new international division of labor
9. commodity chain, core, peripheral
10. social conditions

CHAPTER 10 - Race and Ethnicity

Multiple-Choice

1. b	2. d	3. a	4. d	5. c
6. c	7. d	8. a	9. b	10. b

True/False

1. F	2. T	3. F	4. T	5. T
6. T	7. F	8. T	9. T	10. F

Matching

1. g	2. b	3. j	4. h	5. i
6. d	7. a	8. c	9. f	10. e

Completion
1. race
2. ethnicity
3. minority group
4. assimilation
5. Acculturation
6. cultural pluralism
7. Prejudice, discrimination
8. segregation
9. Institutional discrimination
10. scapegoating

CHAPTER 11 - Sex and Gender

Multiple-Choice

1. c	2. b	3. d	4. a	5. a
6. b	7. b	8. d	9. a	10. d

True/False

1. T	2. T	3. F	4. T	5. T
6. F	7. T	8. F	9. T	10. F

Matching

1. c	2. h	3. d	4. j	5. f
6. a	7. e	8. i	9. b	10. g

Completion
1. Sex, gender
2. patriarchal
3. feminization of labor
4. rape culture
5. Multicultural
6. tokenism
7. sexual harassment
8. social, biological
9. gender roles
10. Classical

CHAPTER 12 - Aging

Multiple-Choice

1. a	2. d	3. c	4. a	5. b
6. d	7. a	8. b	9. a	10. c

True/False

1. F	2. T	3. F	4. T	5. T
6. T	7. T	8. T	9. F	10. T

Matching

1. e	2. j	3. i	4. c	5. a
6. b	7. d	8. h	9. f	10. g

Completion

1. graying
2. Aging, chronological age
3. adult learning
4. biological
5. social age
6. life course
7. generational equity
8. disengagement
9. ageism
10. conflict

CHAPTER 13 - Politics and the State

Multiple-Choice

1. b	2. d	3. d	4. a	5. c
6. a	7. c	8. d	9. b	10. a

True/False

1. T	2. F	3. T	4. T	5. F
6. T	7. F	8. T	9. T	10. F

Matching

1. c	2. e	3. a	4. h	5. j
6. d	7. g	8. i	9. f	10. b

Completion

1. Cold War
2. nation-state
3. law
4. Civil, social, political
5. Rational-legal
6. pluralistic
7. Class dominance
8. authoritarian
9. Direct, representative
10. parliamentary system

CHAPTER 14 - Families

Multiple-Choice

1. a	2. c	3. b	4. d	5. c
6. b	7. a	8. a	9. d	10. c

True/False

1. T	2. T	3. F	4. F	5. T
6. F	7. T	8. F	9. T	10. T

Matching

1. d	2. e	3. i	4. a	5. f
6. j	7. b	8. h	9. c	10. g

Completion

1. family
2. functionalist
3. conflict
4. polyandry
5. nuclear
6. child-minding
7. endogamous
8. baby boom
9. Monogamy
10. cohabitation

CHAPTER 15 - Work and Economic Life

Multiple-Choice

1. a	2. c	3. d	4. a	5. d
6. a	7. c	8. c	9. b	10. a

True/False

1. F	2. T	3. T	4. F	5. T
6. T	7. F	8. F	9. T	10. T

Matching

1. g	2. j	3. f	4. e	5. a
6. c	7. d	8. b	9. i	10. h

Completion

1. Capitalism
2. industrial
3. factories
4. handicraft
5. post-Fordist
6. Conglomerates
7. primary, secondary
8. telecommuting
9. service
10. deskilled

CHAPTER 16 - Education

Multiple-Choice

1. a	2. b	3. b	4. c	5. c
6. d	7. b	8. c	9. d	10. b

True/False

1. T	2. F	3. T	4. T	5. T
6. T	7. F	8. T	9. F	10. T

Matching

1. i	2. f	3. b	4. d	5. a
6. h	7. e	8. g	9. j	10. c

Completion

1. Education	2. Interactionist
3. De facto	4. Functionalist
5. Mass	6. literacy
7. Social conflict	8. Bilingual
9. segregated	10. Functional

CHAPTER 17 - Religion

Multiple-Choice

1. c	2. c	3. b	4. a	5. a
6. d	7. b	8. d	9. a	10. d

True/False

1. T	2. F	3. T	4. T	5. F
6. T	7. T	8. F	9. F	10. F

Matching

1. h	2. f	3. c	4. a	5. g
6. e	7. d	8. i	9. j	10. b

Completion

1. secularization	2. religious economy
3. Religion	4. Animistic
5. church, cult	6. sacred
7. alienation	8. civil religion
9. monotheistic	10. disestablished

CHAPTER 18 - Medicine and Health

Multiple-Choice

1. d	2. c	3. d	4. b	5. a
6. d	7. d	8. c	9. c	10. a

True/False

1. T	2. F	3. F	4. F	5. T
6. T	7. F	8. T	9. T	10. T

Matching

1. f	2. e	3. i	4. d	5. b
6. g	7. j	8. h	9. c	10. a

Completion

1. Health, medicine
2. Preventive
3. sick person
4. medicalization of health
5. Medical care
6. heroic
7. Negative euthanasia, positive euthanasia
8. national health service
9. fee-for-service
10. health care

CHAPTER 19 - The Mass Media in Contemporary Society

Multiple-Choice

1. a	2. c	3. d	4. b	5. a
6. b	7. d	8. d	9. c	10. b

True/False

1. T	2. F	3. T	4. F	5. T
6. F	7. T	8. F	9. F	10. T

Matching

1. i	2. g	3. e	4. h	5. f
6. a	7. c	8. b	9. j	10. d

Completion

1. Class-dominant
2. mass media
3. limited effects
4. mass-mediated
5. culturalist
6. Development communication
7. personalizing
8. technological literacy
9. agenda-setting
10. official sources

CHAPTER 20 - Population, Urbanization, and the Environment

Multiple-Choice

1. d	2. d	3. b	4. a	5. c
6. a	7. b	8. a	9. b	10. d

True/False

1. T	2. T	3. F	4. F	5. T
6. T	7. T	8. F	9. T	10. F

Matching

1. i	2. g	3. f	4. b	5. e
6. j	7. h	8. c	9. a	10. d

Completion

1. agricultural surplus
2. crude birth rate, crude death rate
3. Gemeinschaft, Gesellschaft
4. life expectancy
5. sustainable development
6. human ecology
7. Urban renewal
8. Global warming
9. rural, urban
10. urban growth machine

CHAPTER 21 - *Social Change, Collective Behavior, and Social Movements*

Multiple-Choice

1. a	2. c	3. a	4. d	5. c
6. b	7. c	8. d	9. b	10. c

True/False

1. T	2. F	3. T	4. F	5. T
6. T	7. T	8. F	9. T	10. T

Matching

1. e	2. f	3. j	4. i	5. d
6. a	7. c	8. h	9. b	10. g

Completion

1. differentiation
2. societal change
3. Social movement organizations
4. Reformist
5. grass roots organizing
6. equilibrium state
7. Collective behavior
8. Multilinear evolutionary
9. Rise and fall
10. resource mobilization